WEIGHT TRAINING

About the author

Dr. Rasch purchased his first barbell in 1926 and has been closely involved with this form of training ever since. He took an AA degree at Fullerton District College, California, where he was captain of the wrestling team and a member of Alpha Gamma Sigma honorary scholastic society. After World War II service in the Navy, from which he has since retired as a Lieutenant Commander, he attended the University of Southern California. Here he was captain of the fencing team and obtained a B.A. degree in physical education. Later he added M.A., M.Ed., and Ph.D. degrees to his academic background and was elected a member of the Phi Kappa Phi honorary scholastic society.

Since graduation from the University Dr. Rasch has worked as a corrective therapist at the Veterans Administration Hospital, Los Angeles; Director of the Biokinetics Research Laboratory, California College of Medicine, Los Angeles; and Chief, Physiology Division, Naval Medical Field Research Laboratory, Camp Lejeune, North Carolina, where he also served as physiologist for the U.S. Marine Corps Physical Fitness Academy. He is author or coauthor of several books and well over one hundred articles. Dr. Rasch is a Fellow of the American College of Sports Medicine, a member of the Research Council of the American Alliance for Health, Physical Education and Recreation, an Honorary Life Member of the Royal Air Force School of Physical Training, and is listed in Who's Who in Science. He now lives in California, where he continues his research and writing.

WEIGHT TRAINING

Physical Education Activities Series

Philip J. Rasch

Formerly Chief, Physiology Division
Naval Medical Field Research Laboratory
Camp Lejeune, North Carolina

HONORARY LIFE MEMBER
Royal Air Force School of
Physical Training

SECOND EDITION

Wm C Brown Company Publishers
Dubuque, Iowa

Consulting Editor

Aileene Lockhart
Texas Woman's University

Evaluation Materials Editor

Jane A. Mott
Smith College

Copyright © 1966, 1975 by Wm. C. Brown Company Publishers

Library of Congress Catalog Card Number: 74-29818

ISBN 0—697—07061—1

Printed in the United States of America

Contents

Preface

The reception accorded to the first edition of this book has encouraged the publishers to bring out a revised and enlarged second edition. The President's Council on Physical Fitness and Sports comments, "Until comparatively recent years, weight training was questioned by athletic coaches and physical educators, but it is now almost universally accepted as an effective, efficient means of developing strength, power, endurance, and flexibility." Unfortunately, the excesses of the "body beautiful" cult, the widespread use of drugs by weight trainers, and the fallacious statements featured in the advertising of many of those commercially interested in this form of exercise have caused numbers of physical educators to reject it without regard for its merits.

There is, however, an extensive and growing amount of scientific literature in support of weight training and evaluating its techniques, although many questions yet remain unanswered. This book makes careful use of this material. The references have been especially selected for the information of those seeking an intelligent understanding of the facts underlying the practice, and a list of recommended readings has been supplied for those seeking a broader background in the field than it is possible to present here. A glossary of technical terms, both scientific and popular, and a summary of muscle actions and exercises have been added for convenient reference.

At the same time close attention has been paid to empirical developments in the sport. One such change is the growing interest in weight training for women, especially for women athletes. It must be expected that this trend will continue and expand. Accordingly, a few paragraphs on this topic have been included.

The text has been expanded to permit the addition of more exercises and to clarify certain points which were considered ambiguous in the first edition.

As was stated in the Preface to the first edition, "The 'secrets' of success in weight training are effort, proper diet, sufficient rest. You will get out of it just about what you put into it."

Acknowiedgments

The assistance given by various individuals in the preparation of the second edition of this book is gratefully acknowledged. Particular appreciation is due to John C. Grimek, Editor-in-Chief of *Muscular Development*, and Peary Rader, Editor of *Iron Man*, who responded quickly and fully to every appeal for aid. David P. Willoughby was generous with his time and counsel.

Chris Dickerson. Mr. USA 1968, Amateur Mr. Universe 1973, Professional Mr. Universe 1974. In 1970 Dickerson made history by becoming the first black to achieve Mr. America honors.

Introduction
to weight training

1

Prior to World War II the practice of weight training was confined largely to competitive weight lifters and to professional or amateur "strong men." Athletes in general carefully avoided the weights as their coaches and trainers solemnly warned them that their use would make a man muscle-bound, or "strain his heart," whatever this might mean. The fact that the situation is now so different resulted largely from the pioneering efforts of an Army surgeon, Thomas L. DeLorme, during World War II. Himself a weight lifter, DeLorme was instrumental in introducing the equipment and techniques of this method of training into the Army's orthopedic treatment procedures. The publication of his *Progressive Resistance Exercise* in 1951 marked the beginning of a whole new era in this form of exercise. Hellebrandt hailed his work in these words: "The recent demonstration of how much can be done to expedite the return of normal function by the systematic use of judiciously administered exercise, graded in dosage, is one of the important contributions of the period to human knowledge."[1]

Once the use of weights was approved by the medical profession, the opposition of coaches and physical educators quickly vanished. As a result, this method of training experienced a tremendous growth in public interest. Inevitably this led to specialization as users of weights sought the most efficacious methods of attaining their varied goals. Weight trainers today may be roughly divided into five groups.

Weight Lifters This group comprises an estimated 2,000 competitive lifters in the United States (only 5,088 weight lifters of all types were registered with the Amateur Athletic Union [AAU] in 1974, of whom a large percentage were physique contestants) interested mainly in acquiring the strength, speed, agility, and technique necessary to achieve success in the two Olympic lifts: the two-hand snatch and the two-hand clean and jerk. They usually employ maximal or near-maximal poundages and do not over three repetitions of a given exercise at a time. They may perform single repetitions with rest periods between.

Power Lifters The World Power Lift Federation now recognizes thirteen nations, but the International Power Lift rules differ in some respects from the American rules. Power lifters are concerned almost exclusively with the development of brute strength. They compete in the three power lifts—squat, bench press, and dead lift, contested in that order—in which relatively large amounts of weight may be handled. On occasion the curl or some other form of lifting may be added, and the event is then billed as an Odd Lifts Meet. The training program of power lifters tends toward the use of extremely heavy weights with low repetitions and a large number of sets.

Body Builders Physique contestants are more interested in developing massive musculature and great definition than exceptional strength. They tend to perform several sets of an exercise with a high number of repetitions in each set in an effort to engorge the muscle tissue with blood. Since the relationship between limb girth and strength is relatively small, they are not always as strong as their muscle size might lead the observer to expect. Only rarely are they outstanding athletes.

Athletes Weight training has become extremely popular as a method of preparation for participation in athletics, particularly among weight throwers, football players, and swimmers. These men practice special programs designed by their coaches to develop strength in the movements characteristic of their sport.

Patients Progressive resistance exercises under medical supervision are prescribed to meet a patient's individual needs and are often concentrated on the afflicted area rather than over the entire body. In many cases a body-builder routine is followed as the restoration to normal appearance of an atrophied limb (the so-called cosmetic effect) is often of greater concern to the sufferer than is regaining normal strength.

Of the foregoing, weight lifting, power lifting, and rehabilitation procedures fall outside the scope of this book and will not be considered further. The physiologic principles discussed on the following pages are, however, as valid for those procedures as for any other group.

PHYSIOLOGIC PRINCIPLES OF WEIGHT TRAINING

The bones are in effect a system of articulated levers which are moved by the skeletal muscles. Muscles may be regarded as machines which store chemical energy and convert it to mechanical work in response to impulses conducted by the nervous system. There are approximately 434 muscles, making up about 40 to 45 percent of the body weight, but only about 75 pairs are involved in the general movements of the body. A muscle consists of a large number of cells filled with a liquid protein solution called sarcoplasm. Running through this material are elements called myofibrils. These are the units actually responsible for the process of contraction. The most popular theory is that the myofibrils contain filaments which slide past each other when a muscle contracts or elongates.

There are three types of muscular contraction, each of which has been used as the basis for training systems.

Isotonic   The muscle actually shortens and moves a load, such as a barbell or dumbbell through a distance, thus accomplishing a certain amount of work. Such contractions are also said to be concentric. In practice the weight that can be handled is limited to that which can be moved through the weakest point in the range of motion of a joint.

Isokinetic exercise is a modification of isotonic exercise. It utilizes a machine which controls the speed of the movement. This prevents the dissipation of muscular energy in acceleration and provides resistance which is proportional to the input of muscular force and the alterations in skeletal levers throughout the range of motion. In simpler language, it compensates for the variations in the muscle force which can be developed at various angles of a joint and provides maximal resistance at any angle. These machines are seldom seen in gymnasia at present, but many have apparatus which is somewhat similar in principle but which does not incorporate the speed control factor. These are known as **variable resistance machines** (see fig. 3.9).

Isometric   The muscle is unable to move the load, such as a fixed bar, so that apparently no joint movement takes place. The muscle does not visibly shorten, and technically no work is accomplished even though the muscle is subjected to great stress. This is known as static contraction. The value of this type of exercise has been reviewed elsewhere.[2]

Lengthening   The load forces the contracted muscle to extend, as when a barbell is taken from supports and slowly lowered. This is also a form of isotonic contraction and is known as eccentric contraction in order to differentiate it from concentric movements. In practice it is utilized every time a weight is lowered in a controlled manner during isotonic exercise.

Is the position of this elbow joint appropriate for beginning an exercise movement? Would it be correct if the elbow were flexed at a right angle? At about what speed of movement is mechanical efficiency greatest?

Direction of
Arm Movement

These explanations are somewhat oversimplified and are not completely accurate from the standpoint of muscle physiology. A consideration of the details would take us far astray, however, and for our purposes it is satisfactory to act *as if* they were correct.

Much greater amounts of weight can be handled eccentrically than can be managed concentrically. A great deal of interest is now being taken in this form of exercise. While it is possible that it has certain advantages, the difficulty is that the amount of weight which can be used requires the assistance of training partners or the use of apparatus which is heavy, is expensive, and requires a good deal of space. Another serious question is the extent to which negative exercise reproduces the movements of work or sport.

The amount of force that a muscle can exert depends on the number and size of its myofibrils. It has been believed for nearly seventy years that the number of fibrils cannot be increased by exercise and that growth in muscular size (hypertrophy) results from increases in the sizes of the muscle fibers. However, recent studies have raised some question about the correctness of the belief that the number of fibrils cannot change.

When a muscle is exercised, the material enclosing the cell (sarcolemma) becomes thickened and toughened and the amount of connective tissue increases. There is also an increase in certain chemical constituents of the cell, the blood flow, and the blood pressure. The capillaries (tiny blood vessels) open and dilate, and fluid is attracted from the blood into the tissue spaces. All of this may increase the weight of the muscle by as much as 20 percent. During the rest period following exercise there will be a reduction in the muscle's size, but it will tend to remain somewhat larger than it was before exercise. If the muscle is worked regularly, there will be a permanent increase in the number of capillaries, the ability of the muscle to assimilate nutritive materials will improve, and the size and functional power of the cells will increase.

In general, biochemical studies endeavoring to explain the changes resulting in muscle from training have not been very enlightening. Recently attention has tended to center on the role of the brain and spinal cord. It has been suggested that the power of a muscle depends upon the number of motor units which the nervous system is able to excite in a muscle. Possibly some of them are more easily triggered than are others, and those hardest to arouse can perhaps be brought under voluntary control only as a result of maximal or near-maximal efforts.

Rather obviously the foregoing changes do not appear at the same rate or to the same extent in all individuals, even when they are following identical training programs. Some individuals are what the body builders call "easy gainers" (fig. 1.1); others are "hard gainers." Some men have more fibers in a given muscle than do others, or may have muscles which others lack. Even so, these differences in response to physical activity are not fully understood. By the same token, we have not discovered all the laws underlying successful training. Exercise physiologists, however, are quite confident of the following principles:

1. Strength, endurance, and muscle size increase, within limits, in response to repetitive exercise against progressively increased resistance. This is known as the **overload principle** and requires a psychological approach

Photograph courtesy of Photographic Services, Inc.

Fig. 1.1. Bill Trumbo. Development like this requires that a man have certain natural advantages to begin with and be an "easy gainer" in addition. Trumbo's chest measurement is about 51 inches. Despite the claims in advertisements, relatively few individuals can achieve Trumbo's result.

If your purpose is to gain weight, how should your program differ from one designed to lose weight?

---

committed to all-out efforts. The overload principle is the basis of all programs of weight training.

2. There is an optimal pattern for such exercises. This involves the **intensity** of the stress imposed on the muscle, the **duration** of the training periods, and the **frequency** of the workouts.

3. Exercises which do not involve overloading the body systems have relatively little effect upon performance ability.

4. The critical point is the amount of stress placed upon the body during the given training time.

5. Muscles forced to perform repeated contractions at levels of performance which strain their capacity respond by hypertrophying as well as by increasing their strength.

6. As muscular strength increases, its trainability (ability to respond to repeated contractions of a given force, duration, and frequency by the development of greater strength) decreases.

Actually we do not know as much as we should like to about the best methods of invoking the overload principle, but the physiologists do have several practical hints to offer the weight trainer.

1. A muscle is in position to exert its greatest force when it is somewhat stretched. Each movement should begin from a position in which the joint is fully extended and end with it fully contracted.

2. Mechanical efficiency is greatest at about one-fifth of the maximal speed. The movements should be made slowly and steadily, with the final position held firmly for a few seconds.

3. To permit repetitions the resistance must be sufficiently large to demand a greater-than-normal effort but small enough to require a less-than-maximal effort.

4. There is some evidence that exercise is more effective if done to a definite rhythm.

5. Short, frequent rest pauses should be observed to prevent the muscle from becoming fatigued early in the training session. This gives the heart a chance to drive blood through the muscle, rinsing out waste products and bringing in food and oxygen. The result is a greater work output even though less time is spent in actually moving the weights. In a normal training routine the optimal length of these rest pauses appears to be about three minutes.[3]

SLEEP AND NUTRITION

It seems almost unnecessary to mention that an adequate amount of sleep is necessary if a person is to profit from a training program. It is generally agreed that for the average individual this entails about eight hours a night. The time of day at which one exercises has no known effect on the results, but the weight trainer may find it difficult to get to sleep if he takes a vigorous workout just before going to bed. A man should allow an hour or so for the body systems to return to normal before he retires.

Body builders in particular have a tendency to be faddish in their diet and to consume great quantities of "health foods," "organically grown foods,"* proteins, vitamins, and other dietary supplements. As Kenneth L. Milstead, of the Federal Food and Drug Administration, has remarked, "More people seem to believe more bunk about food and nutrition than any other single topic in the health field and perhaps in any other field."[4] It is, of course, greatly to the financial advantage of those selling such products to promote belief in the need for them—a point which should be kept in mind when reading the magazines devoted to weight training. Many gymnasia carry stocks of fluids such as milk and fruit juice and urge their patrons to drink large quantities of these during their workouts.

Nutritionists recommend that the daily diet include foods from each of the basic seven food groups: (1) milk, cheese, and ice cream; (2) meat, fish, poultry, eggs, dried peas, and beans; (3) bread, flour, and cereals; (4) butter and fortified margarine; (5) potatoes and other vegetables and fruits; (6) leafy, green, and yellow vegetables; and (7) citrus fruit, tomatoes, and raw cabbage. The food intake of Olympic athletes averages around 3,350 calories daily, suggesting that this amount should be ample for the weight trainer unless he is on a massive program to increase his body weight. The major portion should be carbohydrate as it is from this source that the body derives most of its energy. Fats also serve as an important source of energy, but there is some evidence that work efficiency is somewhat less on a high-fat diet than on a high-carbohydrate intake. Protein is necessary for maintenance and growth of the tissues, and in this country the average diet appears to be adequate in this respect.

American weight trainers are notorious for the huge amounts of proteins and amino acid supplements which they ingest. Independent investigators have found that no benefit results from the use of protein supplements[5, 6] or excess vitamins[7, 8] when the subjects are subsisting on a normal

---

*Nutrition experts assert that food grown organically, that is from soil on which no chemical fertilizer or pesticide has been used, has no more nutritional value than does any other, and that in any event the quantity so grown is less than 25 percent of that sold in "organic" stores!

American diet. The concept that the athlete must continually replace proteins in his body has, in the words of Mayer, "been refuted again and again throughout the last hundred years."[9] Additionally, too much protein in the diet may leave an acid residue which imposes an extra load on the kidneys. Massive doses of vitamins A, D, M, and the methyl group have been shown to be harmful. The reason that Central European athletes respond favorably to an increased vitamin intake is simply that their diet is normally deficient in certain of these substances. The authors of *Nutrition for Athletes* state that "Such supplementation in man is expensive and at best probably useless."[10]

There are no miracle foods. Yogurt, blackstrap molasses, brewer's yeast, and similar substances are wholesome and nutritious, but no more so than other products which are usually much less expensive. There is no foundation for the claim that soil depletion causes malnutrition.

It is possible, however, that athletes such as jockeys, boxers, and wrestlers who must stay on a low-calorie diet in order to "make weight" or who must train very strenuously for competition may require more vitamins than they can obtain in their normal dietary intake. What all of this seems to add up to is that if a man lives in a rooming house and gets poorly balanced meals at some local "greasy spoon" or is; "making weight" for competition he may profit by vitamin-mineral supplementation of his food intake. A properly balanced diet is the basis of good nutrition. If one wants to experiment by taking dietary additives, he is certainly privileged to do so. It is his money. He should be careful not to delude himself, however, by attributing to them results which he would have achieved without them.

Drugs

Unquestionably the greatest problem in the field of weight training today is the widespread use of anabolic steroids, the so-called tissue-building drugs. These are synthetic compounds which replicate natural hormones produced in the body and are believed to promote muscular growth. They are sometimes prescribed by physicians to treat metabolic problems which result in reduced ability to assimilate protein. Unfortunately, they may also have highly undesirable side effects. Liver damage, endocrine disturbances, testicular atrophy, and impotency in males have been reported to result from their use. Such organizations as the International Olympic Committee and the AAU disbar any athlete or physique contestant known to have used drugs. Nevertheless, rumors of the utilization of tremendous quantities of these substances by prominent body builders continue to circulate. Their use is also said to be common among football players and field athletes.

Which of these conditions contraindicate a program of weight training?

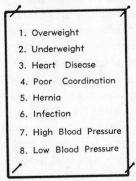

1. Overweight
2. Underweight
3. Heart Disease
4. Poor Coordination
5. Hernia
6. Infection
7. High Blood Pressure
8. Low Blood Pressure

The results of research studies have been conflicting, one problem being the large number of drugs which have been used. The studies are further confused by the fact that some steroid users report that steroids are effective only when accompanied by strenuous training, which may in itself account for some or all of the improvements observed by some users. In view of their doubtful value, the fact that users are debarred from reputable competitions, and the possibility of liver damage and other undesirable side effects, weight trainers should leave anabolic steroids strictly alone.[11]

Alcohol and Tobacco

There is no evidence that moderate consumption of alcohol has any deleterious effect on the development of strength and hypertrophy. Tobacco is somewhat more controversial, especially so far as endurance training is concerned. While there is little in the way of direct evidence that its use is harmful to the weight trainer, the high probability that it is implicated in the development of lung cancer should in itself be enough to discourage its use.

WEIGHT NORMALIZING

The traditional prescription for normalizing the weight is that those wishing to reduce should use low resistance and high repetitions; those seeking to gain should use high resistance and low repetitions. The use of progressive resistance exercises to reduce weight is not very successful unless rigid control of the dietary intake is also instituted. Fat boys have been found to lose some fat as a result of weight training, but there was very little change in total body weight.[12] On the other hand, people who go on a strict diet only may lose muscle tone together with body weight. A combination of increased exercise and decreased food intake appears to be the answer. The addition of running to the training program is usually recommended. The diet should be carefully planned to make sure that it contains sufficient vitamins and minerals while remaining relatively low in calories, but there appears to be no particular advantages to either low-carbohydrate or low-fat diets. Massage, sweat baths, and the like, are of little value other than as a temporary palliative. The second, at least, results merely in loss of water, which is promptly replaced when the person drinks a few glassfuls.

Progressive resistance exercises are, however, more successful when used as an aid in putting on weight, perhaps in part because the exercise makes the subject hungry and he is encouraged to eat more. Hilburn[13] found that over a period of seven months weight-trained boys gained approximately three times as much as did those taking a regular physical education course. His subjects, moreover, did not follow the type of program believed most effective for this purpose.

About 1930 Mark H. Berry introduced the idea of concentrating on a few heavy exercises when endeavoring to gain weight: squats, bent arm pull-overs, dead lifts, supine presses, and two-arm presses, for example. This is now an accepted procedure among weight trainers. Vern Weaver, Mr. America 1963, used only five exercises when trying to increase his body weight: decline presses, high pull-ups, parallel squats, wide grip chins, and straight-arm pull-downs. He used five or six sets of the same number of repetitions, employing as much weight as possible. These programs put on weight but do not by themselves produce attractive physiques. Their proponents insist that the proper way to attain maximum development and shapeliness is to "bulk up, train down."

HAZARDS OF WEIGHT TRAINING

Some years ago Karpovich[14] made a detailed study of the real and alleged hazards of weight training. He found it to be one of the safest of all forms of physical activity. There were, it is true, the usual quota of strains and sprains that must be expected from any form of vigorous exercise, but they were neither exceptionally frequent nor unusually severe when compared with those resulting from other sports. The incidence of hernia and hemorrhoids were much smaller than in the normal male population of the United States, and no cases of damaged hearts were reported. Whether herniae can be prevented by developing the abdominal musculature is a highly controversial question. Some doctors believe that abdominal hernia is evidence of a defect in the muscle structure and that such defects cannot be corrected by exercise. Only two or three fatalities have been attributed to weight train-

From a popular magazine, assemble all of the advice you can regarding exercise, nutrition, drugs, alcohol, tobacco, and fitness. How much of it is questionable?

ing; all occurred when the weight fell on a man during a supine press. More recently Jackson and his collaborators[15] have discussed some additional injuries that have been reported and have suggested safety precautions which should be observed in certain exercises.

The old bugaboo of weight trainers becoming muscle-bound seems to have finally been laid to rest. The condition does exist. It is a limitation of motion which occasionally results when a movement requiring less than the normal range of motion is constantly practiced. Bicycle riders sometimes become muscle-bound in the legs, with the result that they cannot extend the lower leg properly when trying to kick a football. Such restriction of movement is evidence of an improper training program. If anything, progressive resistance exercises tend to increase flexibility beyond normal limits. It is, however, true that the sheer bulk of muscle may reduce the range of a given movement and that muscular men in general have less joint mobility than do slender types. It is also true that each type of athletics tends to reflect a flexibility pattern peculiar to itself. Thus swimmers may exceed weight trainers in the flexibility of certain joints but be exceeded in others by the weight trainers.

There is no evidence that practice of a proper weight-training program will make a man slow or adversely affect his coordination. If anything, the opposite is true, but there seems to be a limit after which further increases in strength are not accompanied by improvement in speed.

As in any other form of activity, overtraining, i.e., exercising to the point of chronic fatigue, will reduce both performance capacity and the body's ability to resist infection.

Most men and women will profit from weight training. There are, however, certain conditions in which it is contraindicated. Those suffering from hernia, high blood pressure, fever, infection, recent surgery, or heart disease should avoid it. It is not possible to "sweat out" a cold, and there is a great deal of evidence that vigorous activity during a period of infection serves to spread throughout the body organisms which might otherwise have been sealed off and rendered relatively harmless. The result may be serious, if not fatal.

WEIGHT TRAINING AND PHYSICAL FITNESS

At this point a note of caution must be sounded. The fact that weight training is unequaled as a means of developing strength does not mean that it is a perfect exercise. A number of studies have shown that its practice results in very little improvement in cardiorespiratory function. In tests of work capacity, weight lifters have been found to be no better than untrained men. If the weight trainer desires to be fit as well as strong, it will be necessary for him to add a good deal of running to his regimen—perhaps something on the order of Cooper's aerobic program.[16] In any event the activity must be vigorous enough so that the heart rate for healthy young men exceeds 150 beats per minute, or no training effect will result.

REFERENCES

1. F. A. Hellebrandt. "Recent Advances in Methods of Hastening Convalescence Through Exercise," *Southern Medical Journal* 39:397-401 (May 1946).
2. Philip J. Rasch. "Isometric Exercise and Gains of Muscle Strength." In *Frontiers of Fitness.* Roy J. Shephard, ed. (Springfield, Ill.: Charles C Thomas, 1971), pp. 98-111.
3. H. Harrison Clarke, *et al.* "Strength Decrements of Elbow Flexor Muscles Following Exhaustive Exercise," *Archives of Physical Medicine and Rehabilitation* 35:560-561 (September 1954).
4. Quoted in Charlotte (N.C.) *Observer,* 11 November 1964.
5. Philip J. Rasch, and William R. Pierson. "The Effect of a Protein Dietary Supplement on Muscular Strength and Hypertrophy," *American Journal of Clinical Nutrition* 11:530-532 (November 1962).
6. Philip J. Rasch, *et al.* "Protein Dietary Supplementation and Physical Performance," *Medicine and Science in Sports* 1:195-199 (December 1969).
7. Philip J. Rasch, *et al.* "Effect of Vitamin C Supplementation on Cross Country Runners," *Sportartzliche Praxis,* 5:10-13 (1962).
8. Jean Mayer, and Beverly Bullen. "Nutrition and Athletic Performance," *Physiological Reviews* 40:369-397 (July 1960).
9. Jean Mayer. "Food Fads for Athletes," *Atlantic Monthly* 208:50-53 (December, 1961).
10. *Nutrition for Athletes.* Washington, D. C.: AAHPER, 1971, p. 30.
11. Lawrence A. Golding. "Drugs and Hormones." In *Ergogenic Aids and Muscular Performance,* William P. Morgan, ed. (New York: Academic Press, Inc., 1972), pp. 379-397.
12. Edward S. Clements. "The Effect of Weight Training on Percent of Total Body Fat and Total Body Weight." Master's thesis, Pennsylvania State University, 1963.
13. Dick Hilburn. "The Effect of Weight Training on Gaining of Weight." Master's thesis, Arkansas State College, 1960.
14. Peter V. Karpovich. "Incidence of Injuries in Weight Lifting." *Iron Man,* 11-7 et seq., September-October 1951. See also *Iron Man* 26:47, (August-September-October 1967.)
15. Frederick E. Jackson, *et al.* "Weight Lifting Injuries." *Journal of the American College Health Association* 19:187-189 (February, 1971).
16. Kenneth H. Cooper. *The New Aerobics.* (New York: M. Evans and Co., Inc., 1970).

Basic
weight training program

2

The man without previous weight training experience begins by following a routine designed to produce all-around development. Experience over the years has resulted in the development of a rather standardizd set of exercises for this purpose. Most of these derive from a book published in Germany in 1907 by Theodor Siebert. Regardless of whose course one takes or whose he may buy, the recommended basic series will be quite similar to the exercises listed and discussed in the pages that follow.

The exerciser first warms up with a series of calisthenics, giving particular attention to stretching the back muscles. It is true that it has not been proved that warm-up is of any advantage in the prevention of injury and that some investigators seriously question its value. However, this is controversial, and it does not appear advisable to recommend its elimination until we are more sure of the facts.[1] The trainer should be careful to keep the body warm during the exercise period, especially when taking his rest pauses. The use of a sweat shirt and sweat pants is highly recommended if the exercise area is not comfortably warm. A temperature of about 68 degrees F. or a little warmer is generally preferred.

In all exercises in which the movement starts with the weight at the chest, the trainer brings it to that position by a simplified version of what is known to weight lifters as the *clean*. He starts with the feet on line, the knees bent, and the bar close to the shins (fig. 2.1). He forcibly extends his knees and pulls the bar as nearly straight upward as is possible, taking a short step forward if necessary to bring the bar onto the upper part of the chest (fig. 2.1). The weights should be loose enough on the bar so that they

Fig. 2.1.   Modified Barbell Clean. **Left,** Proper position for lifting a weight to the chest. Note that the feet are in line with bar, not one foot forward and one back. This subject has his thumb over the bar. Most men prefer to lift it to the chest with the thumb under the bar and make the change before starting the press. **Right,** the weight is started upward by forceful extension of the knees. The lifter steps forward and under the bar as the weight is snapped onto the top of his chest, and his elbows whip under it.

will rotate freely as the arms are snapped under the bar for presses or as the bar rises toward the chest in curling. If they are not, the exerciser will develop sore wrists.

Other than a barbell, the only piece of equipment required for the following exercises is a bench. If the lifter builds his own, it should be not over eleven inches wide, of sturdy construction, and with a wide base which will prevent tipping.

BASIC PROGRAM

Two-Arms Standing Press

The bar is taken to the chest as described, pushed to arm's length overhead, and then lowered to the chest (fig. 2.2). As it passes the head, the weight should move backward a little so that it is in line with the line of gravity of the body. Too far forward or too far backward and control of it will be lost.

Fig. 2.2.   Two-Arms Standing Press.

No spring should be imparted by flexing and straightening the knees (termed a *hitch* by weight trainers), and the exerciser should not lean backward. Most experienced lifters prefer to have the thumbs under the bar and alongside the index fingers while pressing. The press develops the shoulders and the arm extensors: triceps, deltoids, upper part of the trapezius, serratus anterior, and associated muscle groups.

High Pull-Up

The bar is held against the front of the thighs, palms in. It is then pulled up to the chin, the elbows raised as high as possible, and lowered to the starting position (fig. 2.3). The high pull-up develops the shoulders and the arm flexors: trapezius, deltoids, biceps, radialis, brachioradialis, and associated muscle groups.

Fig. 2.3.   Two-Arms High Pull-up.

Have you prepared a mental checklist of safety precautions to guide you as you train? About which items are you most likely to be forgetful or careless unless you are on guard?

Two-Arms Curl (Front Curl)

The bar is held against the front of the thighs, palms out. The elbows are kept close to the sides, and the weight is alternately brought up to the chest and lowered to the starting position (fig. 2.4). The tendency to permit the elbows to move backward or to heave the weight up by bending backward at the waist must be avoided. The exercise can be made in strict form by placing the back against the wall or a post. The bar should be lowered slowly and under full control to take advantage of exercising during the eccentric contraction phase of the movement. It is important that the elbows

Fig. 2.4.   Two-Arms Curl.

be fully extended at the conclusion of this part of the exercise. The two-arms curl develops the arm flexors: biceps, radialis, brachioradialis, and associated muscle groups.

Reverse Curl

This exercise is performed in a manner similar to the foregoing, with the exception that the palms are turned in instead of out (fig. 2.5). It develops much the same muscles as the regular curl, but the exerciser will be able to handle only about two-thirds as much weight due to a change in the mechanical advantage of one of the elbow flexors.[2]

Fig. 2.5.   Reverse Curl.

Some body builders have machine shops bend special curling bars for them. These provide vertical sections for gripping so that curls may be performed with the hands in the intermediate as well as in the front and reverse, positions.

Half-Squat (Parallel Squat)

The bar is brought up to the chest in the usual manner. The knees are first flexed somewhat and then strongly extended. Simultaneously the arms are straightened so that the barbell is hurled above the head. It is then carefully lowered to rest on the shoulders behind the head. There is likely to be an uncomfortable pressure against the vertebrae, and the bars are frequently wrapped in the center with towels or other soft material or bent so as to remove this pressure. The man squats until his thighs are parallel to the floor, keeping his heels on the ground, and then rises, fully straightening the knees (fig. 2.6). The back must be kept as straight as possible, not permitted to round.

Some individuals will find that their quadriceps and hamstrings (semi-tendinosus and semimembranosus) are so tight that they cannot keep their heels on the floor. This forces them into a deep knee bend, with the consequent danger of falling forward. To obviate this a two-by-four-inch plank or a thick barbell plate may be placed under the heels, allowing the lifter to shift his weight backward. The deep knee bend places a little different stress on the quadriceps than does the squat, and some body builders perform both exercises for developmental purposes.

Advanced exercisers sometimes do squats with the barbell held at the collar bones (**front squats**). The back must be kept straight and the head

The center of gravity and the gravity line of the body shift according to the distribution of weight. Analyze several barbell exercises in terms of the adjustments required to maintain stability.

Fig. 2.6.   Half-squat.

Photograph courtesy of York Barbell Company

Fig. 2.7.   Vern Weaver, Mr. America 1963, Using Adjustable Squat Racks.

up, or the lifter will lose his balance. The exercise is said to be excellent for the development of the thigh just above the knees, but many experienced individuals dislike it because breathing becomes difficult. Considerably less weight can be handled in front squats than in regular squats.

Before very long a man will reach the point at which he uses more weight for his squats than he can lift overhead. At that time a pair of adjustable squat racks or standards becomes invaluable (fig. 2.7). These are set at a height low enough so that the bar will clear the horns when the trainer stands up with the weight on his shoulders. After assuming the erect position, he takes two steps backward, performs his exercises, and then steps forward and replaces the bar, looking first to one side and then to the other to make certain that it is in proper position before bending his knees and stepping out from under it.

As originally popularized by Joseph Curtis Hise and Mark H. Berry, this exercise involved a full squat. Full squats and full deep knee bends have been condemned by the National Federation of State High School Athletic Associations and the Committee on the Medical Aspects of Sports of the American Medical Association as potentially dangerous to the internal and supporting structures of the knee joint. It is reported, however, that some professional football teams still use the complete movement. During the forty-odd years that he has been interested in weight training, the writer has never known a man with damaged knees which were attributed to doing full squats or deep knee bends. He has, however, seen a large number of aching backs, particularly when the exerciser has permitted his spine to round to the point that the buttocks were the first part of the body to rise. While there is little experimental evidence to justify avoiding complete knee flexion, there are theoretical kinesiological reasons for hesitating to assume this position. Until the question has been clarified, it seems safer to avoid full squats and deep knee bends. A simple way of gauging the degree of knee flexion is to squat until you are sitting on a bench and then rise again.

Hise and Berry also advocated what they called "**breathing squats.**" The lifter placed the weight on the shoulders, took three to six deep breaths, held the last one, and did a single rapid squat, bouncing up from the deep position, and repeated this procedure for as many repetitions as desired. This procedure is still advocated by some authors, but there are two serious objections to its use: in the first place, bouncing squats are considered to be a cause of knee injuries; in the second place, holding the breath while squatting may induce the **Valsalva maneuver,** which is also undesirable (*see* p. 29).

Squatting movements develop the knee extensors: quadriceps femoris (rectus femoris, vastus lateralis, vastus intermedius, and vastus medialis).

Heel Raises

Following completion of his squats, the lifter retains the weight on his shoulders and raises the heels as high off the ground as is possible (fig. 2.8). He then returns to the starting position. To exercise the involved muscles from several angles, one-third of the repetitions are done with the toes turned out as far as possible, one-third with the toes pointed forward, and one-third with the toes turned in. To increase the resistance, the exerciser may place the toes on the board or plates mentioned, thus increasing the range through which the calf muscles must contract. A popular alternative is to perform the exercise while seated on the bench with the weight resting on the tops of the knees. Most individuals find it necessary to place some sort of padding under the bar. A more advanced approach is to walk up and down a flight of stairs, stepping flat-footed on each tread and raising up on the toes to step onto the next one. Any way it is done, this exercise develops the foot extensors: gastrocnemius, soleus, and associated muscle groups.

Fig. 2.8.   Heel Raises.

Bent Arm Pull-Over

The man lies supine on the bench, with his head at one end, his knees bent so that his feet are on the bench, and his entire back in contact with it. Some swaybacked individuals may not be able to achieve this. The weight is held at the chest with the elbows bent. Keeping the elbows in this position, the arms pivot at the shoulders so that the weight is swung past the head, just brushing the hair, and lowered as far as possible without causing the back to lose contact with the bench. No arching of the back is permitted at any stage of the exercise (fig. 2.9). The weight is then returned to the starting position. The elbows must be kept in, not permitted to swing out to the sides. The exercise may also be done with the reverse grip.

Pull-overs are sometimes performed with the elbows straight instead of bent, in which case considerably less weight is used. This method is not recommended since sooner or later the exerciser will use too much poundage and suffer deltoid strain or an overstretch of the elbow joint capsule. If no bench is available, the exercise can be performed on the floor, but with re-

Fig. 2.9.   Bent Arm Pull-Overs.

duced effect. It develops the upper part of the chest and back: deltoids, pectoralis, latissimus dorsi, teres major, and associated muscle groups.

Straight-Legged Dead Lift (Derrick Lift)

The man bends over at the waist and picks the bar up with the alternate grip, that is, one hand facing in and one facing out. This reduces the likelihood that a heavy weight will pull the fingers open as the gripping muscles tire. The exerciser rises to the erect position and contracts the muscles of the upper back as though trying to pull the shoulder blades together. He then bends over again, lowering the weight to not less than two inches from the floor (fig. 2.10). Some experienced trainers stand on a platform and lower the weight until the bar is at ankle level. It is extremely inadvisable for the novice to try this. When the body is fully flexed, the strain is borne by the ligaments of the back, with little or no assistance from the muscles. Direct injury may result, or the ligaments may be stretched and predisposed to further trauma. Because of the weight there is a tendency for the heels

Fig. 2.10.   Straight-Legged Dead Lift.

to rise off the ground. This must be resisted, or the lifter may end up by falling forward. Blocks may be utilized between the plates and the floor so that the lifter's spine is never fully flexed.

At this point a word of explanation is required. The straight-legged dead lift is simply and solely an exercise for the back muscles. When lifters talk about dead lifting, they refer to a movement in which they bend the knees and lift the weight by contracting the quadriceps. The training routine for this may include the **Hack lift,** which is a squat with the weight held behind the body, as in figure 2.17, instead of placed on the shoulders, and the straddle lift (**Jefferson and Kennedy lift**) in which the lifter straddles a barbell, one foot forward and one back, and lifts it by straightening the knees. These are actually variations of the squat and would have been included under the discussion of that exercise if it had not been necessary to clarify the fact that there are two distinct styles of dead lifting. The same precautions should be observed for the Hack lift and the straddle lift as with squatting; that is, the squat should be made to only the parallel position. The straight-legged dead lift develops the extensors of the back and hip: erector spinae, gluteus maximus, semitendinosus, semimembranosus, and related muscle groups. The Hack and straddle lifts develop primarily the quadriceps.

A variation of the straight-legged dead lift is the "**good morning exercise**" in which the barbell is placed on the shoulders in back of the neck and the exerciser first bends forward and then to each side. Only light weights should be used, and no attempt should be made to fully flex the trunk.

Another excellent exercise for developing the back muscles is the so-called **swan exercise** in which a man lies face downward and then extends his torso. This is shown in figure 3.1. In advanced training a weight may be held behind the head. The main difficulty is finding some way to securely anchor the feet.

Bench Press (Supine Press)

The exerciser lies on his back on a bench with the weight at his chest. The bar is pushed to arm's length and then lowered to the chest (fig. 2.11). It must come to a rest so that it is not bounced up off the chest.

Certain precautions should be taken during this exercise. If the weight gets off to one side, it may cause the bench to tip. For this reason the feet should be placed on the floor in a good position to resist any tendency of the bench to tip. The head should be at the end of the bench so that the weight can be dropped to the floor behind it if it tends to get away from the lifter.

If the supine press is done on the floor, the use of extralarge plates will enable the lifter to roll the weight over his head to the starting position and will protect him if his arms cannot support the weight. If the exercise is performed on a bench, it is strongly recommended that the barbell be placed on some form of supports from which it can be lifted to start the exercise and to which it can be returned upon completion of the presses. Some of the commercially built benches have standards as an integral part of the bench (fig. 2.12), which is a great convenience.

When lifting alone without the use of standards, the exerciser may experience difficulty in getting a heavy weight into pressing position. The

Fig. 2.11. Bench Press. Note that the thumbs are under the bar.

Photograph courtesy of Paramount Gymnasium Equipment Corp.

Fig. 2.12. Supine Bench with Integral Standards.

writer usually pulls the bar hip high, straddles the bench, sits down at the proper spot, lies back, and uses an extension of the knees and toes to heave the bar up to the chest. After the last press it is placed on the upper thighs, he sits up, and then stands with the weight. Men employing heavy weights in this exercise should practice it only when there is a partner available to assist them if they get into difficulties.

The position of the hands may be varied from close together to wide apart in order to work the muscles from different angles. The bench press develops the extensors of the arms, the shoulders, and the chest: triceps, deltoids, and pectoralis major, together with associated muscle groups.

Press Off the Back of the Neck (POBN)

The barbell is placed on the shoulders behind the neck, as for the squat. The exercise may be done standing, which enables you to use a little more weight, but it is usual for the lifter to straddle the bench and sit down. The weight is pressed to arm's length overhead and then lowered to the shoulders behind the neck (fig. 2.13). The head must be kept slightly forward to avoid being hit by the bar as it goes up and down. It is essential that the bar not be dropped on the vertebrae of the neck during the lowering phase of the movement. Care must also be taken to see that the weight does not get too far behind the trainer as he may seriously damage the arms and shoulders in attempting to control it. Many experienced weight trainers consider this the basic exercise for the shoulders.

A variation of this exercise is to alternately lower the bar to the chest and to the shoulders behind the head, thus combining the two exercises into one. The press behind the neck develops the arm extensors and the shoulders: triceps, deltoids, trapezius, and associated muscle groups.

Fig. 2.13.   Seated Press Off the Back of the Neck.

Rowing Motion

The lifter picks the weight up with the palms turned in, bends over at the waist, flattening the back as much as possible and keeping the knees slightly bent, and lets the arms hang down. He then pulls the weights up to the chest, letting the elbows go out so that they are more or less in line with the shoulders, and then lowers it again (fig. 2.14). An effective variation is to pick up the weight with the palms turned outward and bring it to the waist, keeping the elbows as close to the sides as possible. A second variation is to load one end of a barbell, place the other in a corner, straddle the bar, and perform rowing motions in this fashion. Bars are available commercially which are hinged at the floor end. This keeps the base of the apparatus from moving around and damaging the woodwork.

Fig. 2.14.   Rowing Motion to the Chest.

These exercises develop the arm flexors and the back muscles: biceps, radialis, brachioradialis, deltoids, rhomboids, latissimus dorsi, teres major, and associated muscle groups. The first variation has more effect on the latissimus dorsi than do the other two techniques.

Some instructors contend that this position should never be assumed because the long lever and the weight of the trunk, head, arms, and resistance place a great strain on the lower back muscles. While the writer has never heard of anyone being injured while performing rowing motions, the position might be hazardous for those with lower back problems. It is safer if the exercise is performed with the head resting on some sort of a support, which will remove any possibility of back strain.

Wrestler's Bridge

The exerciser starts in the supine position on the floor with his knees bent. He rocks up onto the crown of his head, lifting the buttocks and shoulders from the floor. Men not accustomed to this exercise will find it rather strenuous and are likely to incur a very sore neck if they go at it too vigorously at first. After a period of training without a weight, the exerciser may take a barbell at the chest, thrust it to arm's length as he rocks up on to his head, and lower it again to the chest as he returns to the starting position (fig. 2.15). The exerciser should conclude by assuming the prone position, rolling up on to the crown of the head, and vigorously exercising the neck in this position. A foam rubber pad or some other sort of protection will be needed to keep the scalp from hurting during bridges.

Fig. 2.15.   Wrestler's Bridge.

It is difficult to introduce much in the way of variation in neck exercises unless one buys a head strap from which weights can be suspended or a helmet on which they can be loaded or has a training partner with whom he can perform "bulling" and the other exercises employed by wrestlers. One alternative to the towel exercises frequently used when a partner is available is to hang an inner tube from a hook, place the head inside, and flex the neck muscles in every possible direction against the elastic resistance provided by the tube.

The principal superficial muscle visibly affected by neck exercises is the sternocleidomastoid. Although a large number of associated muscle groups are also affected, they are difficult to differentiate in the living subject.

Many experienced exercisers would probably add two more movements to the foregoing program. It would be just as well not to include them at the beginning of training, but if desired they could be employed after one becomes somewhat accustomed to the exertion of barbell training.

Wrist Curls

The exerciser sits with his forearms on his thighs (fig. 2.16) or on a table. He may, if he prefers, kneel down and use his flat bench in place of a table. He holds a barbell in his hands, palms up. The wrists are alternately extended and flexed through the full range of movement. This exercise may also be performed with the palms down, in which case it is known as the **reverse wrist curl.**

The wrist curl develops the flexors of the forearm: flexor carpi radialis, flexor carpi ulnaris, and associated muscle groups. The reverse wrist curl develops the extensors of the forearm: extensor carpi radialis, extensor carpi ulnaris, and associated muscle groups.

An alternate exercise is the **wrist roller.** A cord is run through a hole drilled through the middle of a short piece of wood or pipe. Weights are suspended from the cord. The exerciser holds the bar in front of him with both hands and rotates it so that the cord wraps around the bar. Such a unit may be easily mounted on a wall if desired. In use, a set in which the bar is revolved in one direction is followed by a set in which it is rotated in the other.

Most people find that the forearms, like the calves, are very difficult to develop. To save possible disappointment, it should be pointed out that while the correlation between the girth of the forearm and the strength of the hand grip is moderately high, development of a strong grip requires movements specifically designed to exercise the finger and thumb flexors in addition to forearm training. These may include grasping a heavy barbell plate and passing it from one hand to the other, carrying a sack of sand or some similar material by one ear, squeezing a sponge rubber ball, taking a sheet of newspaper by one corner and crumpling it up into a tight ball in one hand, or using any of the numerous spring resistance devices to be found on the market.

Shoulder Shrug

The man stands in front of the barbell, squats, grasps the bar with his hands, and stands erect. He then contracts the shrugging muscles, raising the shoulders as high as possible as though trying to touch his deltoids to his ears (fig. 2.17). Most men seem to prefer to work with the palms turned

Fig. 2.16.   Wrist Curls.   Fig. 2.17.   Shoulder Shrug.

Photographs by Gene Mozee

Which body areas are developed by performing a rowing exercise? What precaution can you take to avoid back strain?

---

out. The exercise may also be done with the weight held in front, in which case the palms are usually turned in. In either case the shoulder elevators are developed: trapezius, levator scapulae, rhomboid, and associated muscle groups.

Another excellent exercise is the following.

Triceps Extension (French Press; Triceps Press)

The exerciser stands or sits with the barbell overhead at arm's length as though completing a press. The arms must be close to the ears. The upper arms are kept in this position while the elbows are flexed so that the bar comes down in back of the head. The elbows must be kept perpendicular while the bar is being raised (fig. 2.18). The exerciser will find that there is a decided tendency for them to move outward if the weight is a little on the heavy side.

A variation of this exercise can be done by lying supine on a bench, pressing the weight to arm's length, and then lowering and raising it as described.

Individuals with a large abdomen may wish to add bent knee sit-ups, leg raises, and vee-ups to this program in order to directly exercise their abdominal muscles. The difficulty of the first two movements may be increased by use of an inclined board.

Photographs by Gene Mozee

Fig. 2.18.   Triceps Extension.

BLACKOUTS

Safety precautions to be taken with each exercise have been discussed as the exercise was presented. However, one more point should be mentioned. A man pressing a heavy weight has a distinct tendency to hold his breath. The weight tends to compress the chest, and a high intrathoracic pressure is produced. There is a sudden rise in blood pressure which prevents the return of the venous blood to the heart. This causes an equally sudden drop in blood pressure, and the lifter may become dizzy and feel that he is going to faint. This is known to exercise physiologists as the Valsalva phenomenon (Valsalva was a seventeenth-century Italian anatomist) and may be deliberately used by wrestlers in such holds as the bear hug. A lifter will say that he grayed out or blacked out.

A second danger is that the Valsalva maneuver may increase intraabdominal pressure to such an extent that an inguinal hernia could be produced if there was a preexisting weakness in that area. These considerations suggest that breathing squats may be potentially dangerous to some individuals and are best omitted from the program.

Compton and associates[3] offer three suggestions to prevent blackouts:

1. Avoid hyperventilation before the lift.
2. Stay in the squatting position as short a time as possible.
3. Raise the weight as rapidly as possible to a position where normal breathing can be resumed.

Precisely because blackouts do occur, many writers on weight training lay great stress on detailed instructions in proper breathing. Unfortunately, their advice is frequently contradictory, and Karpovich and Sinning maintain that attempts at "respiratory control in athletics are mostly fanciful but futile attempts to interfere with a wonderfully adjusted breathing mechanism."[4] The general rule is to inhale while contracting the muscles and exhale as they relax.

WEIGHTS AND REPETITIONS

As was explained in chapter 1, the results of a program of progressive resistance exercise seem to depend upon three variables: (1) the amount of stress placed on the muscles, (2) the duration of the exercise periods, and (3) the frequency of the exercise periods. The possible combinations of these three factors and the range of human differences in response to each are so great that researchers have hardly scratched the surface of their possible combinations. We do not even know whether programs designed to produce hypertrophy should differ from those designed to produce strength and, if so, in what ways. If one reads the popular magazines on weight training, he may wonder why more evidence is not cited. The answer is that no publisher of a magazine devoted to weight training and no proprietor of a weight-training gymnasium has ever sponsored a research study which has increased our knowledge of the physiology of activity. As a result of these factors the following suggestions are empirical rather than scientific.

The novice should start with weights which he can handle with comparative ease. As a rough guide for the man not accustomed to hard work the following is offered: press—one-fourth of body weight, curl—ten pounds less than the press, bench press—ten pounds more than the press, back and leg exercises—one-half of the body weight. It will usually be observed that after the first two or three weeks the beginner suddenly finds himself able to handle considerably more weight, especially in such exercises as the bench press. This does not mean that his strength has greatly increased in that short period. It results from the fact that he has learned how to balance the weight, how to relax antagonistic muscles, and otherwise how to improve his coordination. At that time the amounts of weight employed in the various exercises will need to be adjusted upward. Thereafter he should be able to remain on a schedule for changes in weights and repetitions.

The general rule is that a man begins with five or six repetitions of each exercise for the arms and ten or twelve for the back and legs. He works out three days a week: Monday, Wednesday, and Friday. (The idea of a rest every other day appears to have been one of Alan Calvert's contributions to weight training.) It should be anticipated that with proper warm-up, rest pauses, and the like, the exercise period will approximate two hours. Each Monday he adds one repetition to the arm exercises and two to the back and leg exercises. After a week of ten or twelve repetitions for the arms and twenty or twenty-four for the back and legs, he increases the weights for the former by five pounds and for the latter by ten pounds, and returns to the original five/six and ten/twelve repetitions. There is, of course, an end point to any progression. Sooner or later there will come a time at which the increment must be smaller than suggested. Eventually they may be measured in ounces.

The foregoing method is known as the **double progressive system,** since both the weights and the number of repetitions are increased at regular intervals. The older **single progressive system** consisted of keeping the repetitions at a given number but adding weight as frequently as possible. It is seldom seen today except among competitive lifters. Less popular now than some years ago is the **"1001 Exercises"** system. This assumes that the best way to develop muscles is to exercise them in a large number of different ways so that every fiber is stressed. The training program may be changed almost weekly in order to gain new approaches. For some reason this does not seem to work out as well as one would expect. Quite possibly the number of exercises included in such a program necessitates a reduction in the intensity of the effort put into each one. Generally speaking, greater development seems to result from more concentrated methods, but this system may have some advantages for those seeking extreme definition of muscle.

Burns

Some weight trainers follow their initial repetitions with a series of rapid half-contractions. This produces a burning sensation in the muscle—hence the name. They believe that this forces an additional amount of blood into the muscle and causes a greater increase in size. This sort of thing is best left to the advanced exerciser.

PROGRAM EVALUATION

To a large extent any program, basic or advanced, can be evaluated by the question How do you feel the next morning? If you are unable to sleep, wake up exhausted, and have to drag yourself out of bed and through the day, you are probably overtraining. All too often the beginner finds his measurements shrinking and his strength decreasing. In desperation he drives himself to still greater exertion. This is precisely the wrong thing to do. A Mr. America may have to train every day if he is to keep in top competitive condition, but it is during the rest periods that his muscles build up. Proper rest is just as important as is proper exercise. The forty-year-old man may find that two workouts a week suit him best. Some experienced trainers recommend that every six weeks of hard training be followed by one week away from the weights. When training is resumed, the exercise program is changed. If nothing else, this breaks up the monotony, and a man goes back to his workouts rested and with renewed enthusiasm.

WEIGHT TRAINING FOR WOMEN

Sooner or later most weight trainers, seeing a vast important in their own bodies, endeavor to persuade their girl friends or wives that they too would profit by taking up this activity. (Those desiring research support for the benefits of weight training for young women are referred to the thesis by MacIntyre.[5]) Many girls resist for fear that they will become masculine in appearance. This fear is groundless. In recent years most beauty queens in California have trained with weights.

Often the man itself is uncertain just what sort of a program women should follow. The answer is that it should be in general identical with that pursued by the man—one devoted to developing the whole body, not just working on problem areas. There is, for example, no such thing as "spot reduction." The average female's strength is about two-thirds that of a male's, due largely to her smaller body size. Keeping this in mind, the girl should train with weights that are relatively heavy for her and with progressively increased resistance. Women athletes, of course, will have the benefit of coaches to devise programs especially suited to their needs.

As the trainer performing the exercise in figure 2.18 gains in strength, how can he alter the exercise in order to keep the overload principle operative?

If problems persist after a basic training period has been completed, specialized exercises may be added to the program. Table 2.1 lists the most common feminine figure faults and appropriate exercises to overcome each.

Table 2.1.   Most Common Feminine Figure Faults
and Appropriate Exercises

Fault	Exercise
Conspicuous collar bones and/or undersized bust	Bent arm pull-overs; flying exercise; bench press with dumbbells
Large abdomen	Bent knee sit-ups; vee-ups; all forms of side bends and twists
Flabby thighs	Squats; leg press; front, side, and back leg raises; lunges and stair climbing with barbell on shoulders; leg flexion and extension with iron boot
Underdeveloped calves	Heel raises; walking on the toes with barbell on shoulders

REFERENCES

1. B. Don Franks. "Physical Warm-up." In *Ergogenic Aids and Muscular Performance*. William P. Morgan, ed. (New York: Academic Press, Inc., 1972) pp. 159-191.
2. Philip J. Rasch. "Effect of the Position of Forearm on Strength of Elbow Flexion." *Research Quarterly* 27:333-337 (October, 1956).
3. D. Compton et al. "Weight-Lifters' Blackout." *Lancet* 2:1234-1237 (1 December 1973).
4. Peter V. Karpovich, and Wayne E. Sinning. *Physiology of Muscular Activity*, 7th ed. (Philadelphia: W. B. Saunders Co., 1971), p. 150.
5. Christine MacIntyre. "Effect of a Weight Training Program on Body Contours of Young Women 18 to 22." Microcarded Master's thesis. University of California, Los Angeles, 1967.

Advanced
training methods

3

There are no secrets in weight training. Generally speaking, a man gets out of it just about what he puts into it. There is, however, a tremendous variation of potential development from individual to individual. One man will thrive on a training program which will reduce another to a state of chronic fatigue. A system that works wonders for one body builder may prove less than satisfactory for another. In part this may depend upon the stage of training of the persons concerned, but a few individuals never seem to respond to any form of training. Difficult cases have to combine open-mindedness and readiness to experiment with willingness to stick with a given schedule long enough—say three months—to give it a chance to show its potentials for them. Then if it does not seem to be producing the desired results, they should try a different approach.

After some months on the basic course described in Chapter 2, an exerciser will reach a point at which he decides that he is no longer progressing as fast as he should. This is an indication that the time has come to switch to advanced training methods. Two different approaches are possible: changes in the system of training and in the use of apparatus. These will be discussed in that order. The reader may wonder why, if there are superior systems, he should not start with them instead of wasting time on a basic program. All advanced training methods depend upon one basic principle: increasing the amount of stress placed upon the body within the given training period. The beginning weight trainer is no more ready for these levels of work than is a college wrestler prepared for competition on the first day of team workouts. Only rarely should a man consider advanced training

---

Plan a program of weight lifting designed to keep yourself in shape. What reasons support your choice of the activities selected?

---

methods until he has completed six months or more on the basic program. Even longer may be advisable. Joe Abbenda, who has held the Mr. America and both the amateur and professional Mr. Universe titles, has stated that he spent the first two years of his training performing just three exercises: the squat, the dead lift, and the bench press.

SYSTEMS OF TRAINING

In chapter 2 we discussed the single progressive and double progressive systems. There are, however, several others. The most popular are described here:

Light and Heavy System

The trainer starts out with a weight considerably lighter than his maximal, does a few (perhaps three) repetitions, stops, adds more weight (perhaps five pounds), and performs a few more repetitions, continuing this procedure as long as he can. Toward the end of such a series the amount of weight added may be decreased to the point that it consists of no more than a couple of iron washers, and the number of repetitions may be decreased from three to two, and finally to one. This was the method followed by the Egyptians during the years that they were the world's best weight lifters and is still advocated today by many men whose main interest is in the development of strength.

Heavy and Light System

This procedure has been popularized by the lifters at York, Pennsylvania. The individual starts off with the maximum weight which he can handle for a given number of repetitions, completes these, takes off some weight, and again repeats a maximal number of repetitions, repeating this procedure as long as he can continue. The basic principle is to keep the muscle working against near-maximal resistance even though fatigue is reducing its capacity for performance. There is some evidence that this method of training is more effective than is the light and heavy system. This technique is very popular in rehabilitation work where it is often referred to as the Zinovieff or the Oxford technique.

A variation of this program is to have fellow trainers remove approximately 20 percent of the weight as soon as the trainer falters, so that the exercise continues without interruption. This is known as the **multipound-age system**. It was introduced by Henry J. Atkin in England about 1949 and is more popular there than in the United States. One difficulty with it is that requires a fairly large assortment of weights in order to make the changes, and at least three men must work out together.

Blitz Program

The exerciser trains five days a week, but works on only one group of muscles on each day. For instance, Monday might be devoted to the arm flexors, Tuesday to the arm extensors, Wednesday to back and chest exercises, Thursday to the legs, and Friday to the abdomen. Bruce Page recommends that each exercise be performed for five sets of six repetitions each. The goal is to keep a limited muscle area flushed with blood for a prolonged period. Like the every-hour-on-the-hour system, this is a very vigorous program and is usually followed for a comparatively short time. In effect it is a split routine carried to an extreme. Usually comparatively light weights are employed.

Cheating Exercises

These exercises were introduced to American weight trainers following Berry's observations of the training methods of the German Olympic Weight-Lifting Team at Los Angeles in 1932. They consist of using more weight than can be handled in strict form and then employing movements of other parts of the body (what kinesiologists term **synergistic muscle action**) to get the weight past the sticking point. In the two-hands curl, for instance, the problem is usually to get the weight started. Performed as a cheating exercise, the man leans forward at the waist and starts the lift by swinging his upper body backward. In the press he would first swing his hips backward and then start the weight upward by swinging them forward. The essential point is that the movement is performed in proper style once the sticking point is surmounted.

This form of exercise has much to recommend it as it enables the man to provide maximal resistance to the muscle through that portion of the range of motion in which it is strongest, whereas otherwise the resistance afforded is actually controlled by the amount it can handle through the range wherein it is weakest. Further, it simultaneously exercises other parts of the body which would be involved to only a relatively small degree if the strict style were followed. The value of the exercise is lost if the synergistic movements are performed in such a way as to merely throw the weight through the movement. Properly performed, this is an extremely effective system.

Circuit Training

Morgan and Adamson[1] and Hellebrandt and Houtz[2] advanced the theory that a man could improve his strength and endurance by a program which placed the emphasis on a reduction of the time required to complete a given exercise program. A circuit consists of a number of stations, at each of which one exercise is performed. The loads should be about one-half of the man's maximal effort. He is given a trial to see how long it takes him to complete this series of exercises and is then assigned a target time approximately one-third faster than his recorded time. As soon as he can complete the circuit in this time, the loads are increased, he is again timed, and a new target time is established. Variations are possible in the number of exercises and the number of times he goes around the circuit. The circuit may be **biased** to give specialized or increased amounts of work to certain muscles or areas of the body.

This form of training is popular with athletes and the armed forces of the world (fig. 3.1) as it provides the cardiorespiratory stress which is lacking in most systems designed to develop strength.

Compound Exercises

Men pressed for time may combine two exercises into one. For instance, they may do a curl or a reverse curl and continue the movement on into a press, or a press while executing a squat, or a deep knee bend followed by a heel raise, or a bent arm pull-over followed by a press. This may have been the ancestor of the superset system, but possesses the disadvantage that the weight used will be governed by the amount which can be handled in the movement in which the man is weaker.

Peripheral Heart Action (PHA or Sequence) System

This is the most recent system to find favor with weight trainers and is the opposite of the blitz program. The emphasis here is on keeping the blood in constant circulation through the muscular system so that it will bring a steady supply of oxygen, nourishment, and buffers to a given area and remove metabolic wastes and prevent congestion. This is done by arranging groups of five or six exercises, called a **sequence,** in such a way that each exercise affects a different part of the body. For example, a sequence might consist of the press, rowing motion, sit-up, heel raise, and dead lift. Each exercise is performed for eight to ten repetitions, and each sequence is repeated two to five times. The exerciser then goes on to another sequence, performing in all a total of four to six sequences. No rest is taken between

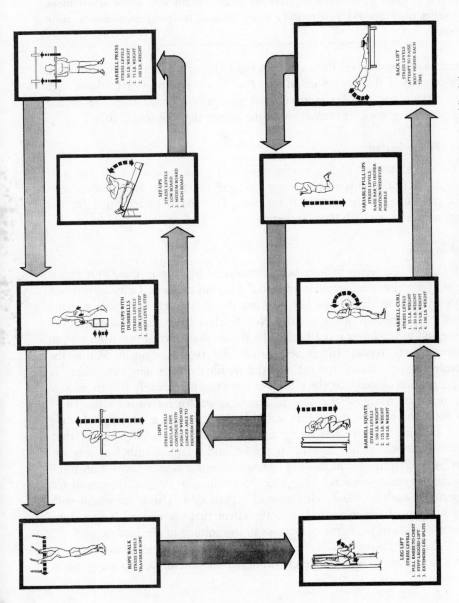

Fig. 3.1. Circuit used at U.S. Marine Corps Physical Fitness Academy, Quantico, Virginia.

There are certain benefits inherent in circuit training that frequently are missed in systems devised to increase strength. Do you know what these benefits are? Should you modify your present training program to gain them?

exercises or sequences; the man goes right through one and into the next. Proponents of this system claim that they can take a heavier workout with less fatigue and quicker recovery, but generally concede that it is better adapted for producing strength and definition than muscular size.

Rest-Pause System

The weight trainer does a single movement, using close to his maximal weight, rests a minute or two, does a second movement, rests, and repeats this process until the muscle is fatigued. This seems better fitted for the production of strength than hypertrophy.

Set System

The use of sets seems to have been introduced by Hise in the 1940s and is now by far the most popular advanced training method. Originally it was a variation of the heavy and light system, that is, in each set lighter weights than in the previous one were used. Now the trend is to keep the weight the same and to use fewer repetitions. The trainer does several repetitions of an exercise, rests, repeats the exercise, rests, and repeats it again. While the number of repetitions in a set and the number of sets may vary, there is some good evidence that three to four sets of approximately five to six repetitions each comprise the optimal combination for increasing strength.[5, 6] In order to conserve space, this would be indicated in a training schedule as 3 x 6, that is, three sets of six repetitions each. It seems doubtful that heavy loads with a few repetitions per set and a large number of sets are any more effective for improving strength than are lighter loads with more repetitions and fewer sets.[6] MacQueen[7] recommends four or five sets of ten repetitions each for the development of hypertrophy. This is consistent with the findings of scientific studies to the effect that exercises of longer duration are followed by a greater increase in the volume of the muscle.

    Training Poundage Goals.   Steiner[8] has proposed minimum poundage goals for advanced weight trainers using the set system. Details are given in Table 3.1.

Supersets

A set of exercises for one group of muscles is followed immediately by a set for their antagonists. A variation of this is known as **super multiple sets** and

Table 3.1.   Training Poundage Goals

Exercise	Goal
Two-hands press	Body weight less 40 lbs.
Press off the back of the neck	Body weight less 50 lbs.
Bench press	Body weight plus 20 lbs.
Rowing motion	Body weight plus 20 lbs.
Squat	Body weight plus 75 lbs.
Straight-legged dead lift	Body weight plus 50 lbs.

consists of performing three sets of an exercise for one group of muscles followed by the same number of sets for their antagonists. A short rest is taken between sets. In the considered opinion of Peary Rader, this is the most effective system for building the arms. These are extremely fatiguing methods and are recommended only for experienced men.

Split routines

Individuals pressed for time or on a very heavy training program may pursue a split routine. This means that on one day they exercise only the upper body and the next day only the lower body. It is, of course, necessary to work out six days a week. Opinion is divided as to the desirability of this method. Some feel that it has no advantages over a normal program; others contend that a split program enables them to accomplish more exercise than they would otherwise without inducing overfatigue.

There is little in the way of research material to indicate the comparative values of these programs and their numerous variations. Men like John Grimek developed some of the great physiques of our time before blitz programs and other such methods were introduced. If the contemporary programs do nothing else, however, they introduce some welcome variety into training schedules which might otherwise become boring. Perhaps they serve to retain the interest of weight trainers who would otherwise fall by the wayside. Certainly they provide a fertile field of study for men interested in the scientific side of exercise.

Even with the best of systems the average man may anticipate that the forearms and calves will prove difficult to develop, so he should not become discouraged if they fail to respond as promptly as he would like. There is in fact a developing scientific opinion that different groups of muscles respond differently to exercise. When we finally attain a truly scientific method of training, it is quite likely that we will use different techniques for different muscle groups.

USE OF APPARATUS

During the last few years the weight trainers have developed a great deal of apparatus to help them attain maximal strength and hypertrophy. Some of it is ingenious, but complicated. Fortunately some of the most effective is also the most simple and can be built by almost anyone. There is available from *Iron Man Magazine* a helpful pamphlet entitled *Twenty Simplified Plans of Weight Training Equipment*[9] which provides dimensions, bills for materials, and the like. The apparatus described can easily be constructed by any "hammer mechanic."

Incline Bench (Slant Board)

One of the simplest and most common pieces of apparatus seen in weight-training gymnasia is the incline bench (fig. 3.2). This was originally designed so that the angle of the incline could be changed. The idea was that if it were slowly increased the trainer would eventually be able to press in the standing position the same amount which he had originally used in the bench press. This method of training seems to be largely forgotten. Most boards are now either built on a 45-degree slant or put in that position and left there so that the exerciser is in effect working in a position midway between supine and standing. It is especially valuable for pressing and flying motions, although curls and numerous other exercises can be performed on it with profit.

When a strap is fixed across the top so that the man can insert his feet under it and place his head at the bottom, it is referred to as a decline board. Most people find a 45-degree incline too extreme for them and prefer to use one with a lesser gradient. Pressing done in this position is especially popular as it imparts a different stress to the pectorals and contributes to their full development.

Hopper

The hopper was originated by Hise. It is seldom seen in the gymnasium today, but in the writer's opinion is an extremely valuable aid. The construction is diagramed in figure 3.3 and can be built quite easily. In use the man stands in the center, lifts the barbell, and lets it come down hard so that the weight rebounds slightly. The hopper raises the bar high enough so that the period during which the upper body "hangs from its ligaments" during dead

Photograph courtesy of Iron Man Industries

Fig. 3.2.   Adjustable Incline Bench.

Fig. 3.3.   Diagram for Construction of a Hopper.

lifting is eliminated. This protects the lifter from back injuries. At the same time the amount of weight which can be handled is considerably increased.

The disadvantages of this piece of apparatus are the thunderous noise and the shock which results when a heavy weight is banged down on it. It certainly has no place in an upstairs room if one has any regard for the plaster on the ceiling below. A rather ingenious solution to this problem was used by some of the earlier competitive dead lifters. These men dug a hole in the ground and stood in it while lifting the barbell. This enabled them to use a weight too heavy to be handled in the normal manner. As their strength increased, they began to fill in the hole, eventually arriving back at floor level. The basic idea, of course, is similar to the use of the adjustable incline board as a connecting link between the flat bench and the standing press. It would seem that the same thing could be more easily accomplished by lifting the weight from blocks and gradually decreasing their height.

Lat Machine

Probably the most popular piece of apparatus in the average gymnasium is the latissimus dorsi machine because of its demonstrated value in developing those muscles and thus producing the **V**-shape so admired by body builders. Normally the men kneels or sits in front of it and pulls the bar down to his shoulders behind his head, although it is sometimes pulled down in front of the head as shown in fig. 3.4. There are differently shaped bars, and they are said to have different effects on the muscles. Another

Is this muscle one of the more or less easily developed? Which two muscles are the most difficult to develop?

Fig. 3.4. Lat Machine.

Fig. 3.5. Leg Press Machine.

popular exercise is to keep the elbows extended and swing the bar down in front of the body as though the arms were pivoted at the shoulders. A triceps extension movement is often done. The bar is grasped with the forearms parallel to the floor. The elbows are then fully extended, with every effort being made to prevent any movement of the upper arms or body.

As his strength increases, a light man may find the weight tends to lift him up, and he may require a fixed seat with a belt attached to hold him in place.

Leg Press Machine

One of the finest pieces of apparatus for developing the legs is the leg press machine (fig. 3.5). While it cannot be seen in figure 3.5, there is a small triangular platform which fits under and raises the hips, thereby flattening the lower back and reducing the chance of injury. It develops much the same muscles as does the squat, but a great deal more weight can be handled with this apparatus than in the squat as it is not necessary to lift the body in addition to the weight.

A popular exercise for the calves performed with this machine is shown in figure 3.6. The exercise is known as the **donkey raise** and is illustrated so clearly that no explanation is required. The exercise can also be performed in the inverted position.

Fig. 3.6.   Donkey Raises.

Knee Flexion and Extension Machine

The uses of this machine are so well shown in figure 3.7 that there is no necessity for a description. Its great virtue is that it furnishes resistance throughout the range of movement. If prone knee flexion is performed with an iron boot, gravity takes over once the weight passes the perpendicular, and it then becomes a matter of contracting the extensors to keep it from

Fig. 3.7.   Knee Flexion and Extension Machine.

Photographs courtesy Iron Man Magazine

Photographs courtesy of Paramount Gymnasium Equipment Corp.

falling on the exerciser. There is no other piece of apparatus known to the writer which quite replaces this item.

Calf Machine

The calf machine comes in a large range of designs, but all are essentially ways of conveniently resting the resistance on the shoulders while doing heel raises. The example shown in figure 3.8 is one of the simpler models; some are engineered to work through a lever system. In any case they are excellent devices for working these hard-to-develop muscles through their full range of movement.

Fig. 3.8.   Jack Delinger, Mr. America 1949 and Mr. Universe 1956, Exercising on a Calf Machine.

Variable Resistance Machines

An example of a popular variable resistance machine is seen in figure 3.9. As has been explained earlier (see p. 3), this apparatus is designed to afford a relatively constant degree of resistance throughout the entire range of motion of a joint. When using a barbell the exerciser is limited to the amount of weight that can be moved through the point of the poorest mechanical advantage. At all other points the muscles are exercised at suboptimal levels. The variable resistance feature automatically compensates for changes in mechanical advantage and maintains a relatively stable load-to-strength ratio.

Almost any standard weight-training exercise can be practiced on these machines, and a number of men can work out at one time. The fact that the weights are under constant control is an important safety factor.

Isometric Rack

The isometric rack is sometimes called the **power rack**. This name is highly inappropriate. Technically, power is equal to the work accomplished divided

Fig. 3.9. A Popular Type of Variable Resistance Apparatus. The cantilevers to which the weights are attached are designed to afford optimal resistance at point in the range of motion of a joint as alterations occur in the mechanical efficiency of the levers and the muscles which operate them.

Photograph courtesy of Universal Athletic Sales

Fig. 3.10. Tommy Kono, who has held World Weight Lifting Championships at two different weights, practicing isometric exercise at the sticking point in the two-hands press.

Photograph courtesy of John Grimek

by the time required to do it. In isometric exercise the bar is not moved, and no work is accomplished. While some use is made of isometric exercise as an adjunct to weight training, it is difficult to determine the extent to which it is actually employed. When it is utilized, the most common procedure seems to be to determine the sticking point in a given exercise. A bar is then fixed at this level, and the man exercises against it isometrically in hope of developing his strength to the extent that he can move an actual weight through this point (fig. 3.10). The writer knows of no research in which this method of training has been evaluated, and claims for its benefits must be treated with caution. This piece of apparatus may also be used to confine a barbell to a given range of movement, thus reducing the possibility of injury.

Those who desire to experiment with the isometric rack as an aid in sports training might be interested in using a system such as the one devised by Bruno[10] for football players. The exercises consist of the squat, dead lift, bench press, and upright rowing motion. On Monday they are performed with the bar at a low level, on Wednesday with the bar at an intermediate level, and on Friday with the bar at a high level. Two sets of three-to-five repetitions are performed. The great drawback to this form of training is that it does nothing to improve cardiorespiratory condition.

REFERENCES

1. R. E. Morgan and C. T. Adamson. *Circuit Training*, 2nd ed. (London: G. Bell and Sons, Ltd., 1961).
2. F. A. Hellebrandt and S. J. Houtz. "Methods of Muscle Training: The Influence of Pacing." *Physical Therapy Review* 38:319-322 (May 1956).
3. Edward K. Capen. "Study of Four Programs of Heavy Resistance Exercises for Development of Muscular Strength." *Research Quarterly* 27:132-142 (May 1956).
4. Richard Berger. "Effect of Varied Weight Training Programs on Strength." *Research Quarterly* 33:168-181 (May 1962).
5. Patrick O'Shea. "Effects of Selected Weight Training Programs on the Development of Strength and Hypertrophy." *Research Quarterly* 37:95-102 (March 1966).
6. R. T. Withers. "Effect of Varied Weight-Training Loads on the Strength of University Freshmen." *Research Quarterly* 41:110-114 (March 1970).
7. I. J. MacQueen. "Recent Advances in the Technique of Progressive Resistance Exercise." *British Medical Journal* 4878:1193-1198 (November 20, 1954).
8. Bradley J. Steiner. "Choosing Your Correct Poundages." *Iron Man* 33:22 et seq. (January 1974).
9. Stephen Kazan. "20 Simplified Plans of Weight Training Equipment" Alliance, Nebraska: *Iron Man Magazine*).
10. Frederick W. Bruno. "Power Rack Training for Football." *Athletic Journal* 53:28 et seq. (September 1972).

The use of dumbbells

4

Nearly any exercise that can be done with a barbell can be duplicated with dumbbells. The latter, however, frequently have special advantages of their own. Often they create more stress on the muscles than do the barbells. In the press, for instance, the even distribution of the weight on a barbell tends to inhibit any tendency for the bar to move sideways, whereas dumbbells require a powerful contraction of the shoulder muscles to keep them from dropping to the sides. Few individuals can press as much with two dumbbells as they can with one barbell. In the curl the bar inhibits the tendency of the biceps to turn the forearms into a supine position. Most men, nevertheless, prefer barbells to dumbbells. Among the older weight trainers the latter have a reputation for making a man stiff. The reason for this was never clear to the writer, and he has not personally experienced this effect.

In the routine exercises such as the press and the curl most trainers seem to prefer "alternate" exercises, that is, one arm goes up as the other is coming down. Usually more weight can be handled in this way than when both are pressed or curled together, and it is easier to concentrate on the movement being made. There is, however, a decided tendency to use body movements to aid the arms. To avoid this many men prefer to do such exercises either sitting or on the incline bench. While the writer has no scientific evidence to back up his opinion, he has a strong impression that a number of body builders famed for the girth of their arms spend an inordinate amount of time working with dumbbells either seated or on the incline bench.

What factors govern the choice between barbells and dumbbells? Is there a difference in the weight that can be handled? Which equipment is more popular?

While barbell exercises can be done with dumbbells, it does not follow that the reverse is true. There are a number of dumbbell exercises which cannot be performed with a barbell. Some of the more popular are described here.

Front Raise

The man stands erect, with the dumbbells resting against the front of the thighs, elbows extended, palms in, raises them to shoulder height directly in front, swings the arms back until they are parallel to the shoulders, and then lowers them to the sides. Next he lifts them back to shoulder height, swings them to the forward position, and lowers them to the original starting position (fig. 4.1). The elbows must be kept extended throughout the exercise.

Photographs by Gene Mozee

Fig. 4.1.   Front Raise.

A variation is to start the movements by raising the arms until the dumbbells are overhead and then lowering them to shoulder height. Another variation is to lean forward at the waist, the arms hanging down, and then raise the dumbbells as high as possible while keeping them in line with the shoulders (fig. 4.2). This is known as the **bent over lateral raise.** These exercises develop the shoulders and upper back: deltoids, supraspinatus, upper trapezius, and associated muscle groups.

A **side raise,** done while lying on one side on a bench, is also popular.

Fig. 4.2.   Bent Over Lateral Raise.   Fig. 4.3.   Dumbbell Swing.

Photographs by Gene Mozee

Dumbbell Swing

The exerciser bends over with the elbows extended and the dumbbell held between the legs with both hands, knees semiflexed. The dumbbell is swung upward, keeping the elbows extended. The feet do not move, but the man comes to a semierect position. One variation is to swing the dumbbell in one hand, with the free hand placed on the knee. The hands may be changed at the top of the swing so that the swing is made with each hand alternately. Another is to swing the dumbbell up and to squat or to take a lunging step forward at the same time. A dumbbell may be used in each hand, starting them outside of the legs and swinging them both at once.

While these variations affect the body in somewhat different ways, the general purpose is to develop the muscles of the lower back: the spinae erectors and associated muscle groups. The shoulders, especially the deltoids, also benefit. Dumbbell swings must not be done until the man is well warmed up, or back strain may be suffered.

Flying Motion

The exerciser is supine on a flat bench, arms extended in line with the shoulders but partially flexed at the elbows. The arms are crossed over the chest and then returned to the starting position. The arms are alternated each time they are crossed so that one is uppermost one time and the other the next.

A variation of this is to do the exercise with the elbows straight. This is known as the **supine** or **straight-arm lateral raise** and is open to the same

Fig. 4.4.   Flying Motion.

objection as is the straight-arm pull-over. Either form, however, develops the shoulders and upper chest and back: deltoids, pectoralis major, middle trapezius, and associated muscle groups.

Hise Deltoid Exercise

The exerciser grasps a doorway or some other brace with one hand. The arm is extended, but with most individuals there is a slight bend in the elbow, and the torso is usually at a slight angle backward. The exercise starts with the weight overhead, elbow extended and upper arm close to the head, as though a press had just been completed. The dumbbell is lowered rapidly to the shoulder and at once rebounded to arm's length. The supporting arm prevents body movement which might aid in the exercise and relieves the man from any worries about retaining his balance. The collars must be set up tightly as the rapid rebounding will tend to loosen them. As the name indicates, this exercise is designed primarily to influence the deltoids, but the triceps and upper shoulder muscle groups in general benefit from it.

One-Arm Push

The man stands erect with the dumbbell at the shoulder and the opposite foot a little advanced. As the weight is pushed up, the hand turns so that the palm is rotated forward, almost on a line with the shoulders, the knees are flexed a little, the torso bends forward and is supported by the free forearm coming to rest on the knee of the advanced leg. The hip on the lifting side must be thrust backward as a counterbalance. Most lifters find it easier to control the weight if they look upward at it. Many prefer to put their free hand on the advanced knee as they begin to lean forward and then slide the forearm across it. In this way they are never left unsupported. The weight is kept a little back of the center line of the body.

This exercise is excellent for practically all of the muscles of the shoulder and back as well as for the arm extensors. In an advanced form this movement develops into the **bent press.** This is now an almost forgotten lift, but when it was in its heyday a good bent presser could put up as much weight with one arm in this style as he could press with both arms in the usual manner.

Side Bend

The exerciser stands erect, the dumbbell at his side. He bends as far to that side as possible and then returns to the erect position. This movement exercises the lateral flexors: abdominis oblique, erector spinae, and associated muscle groups.

Wrist Abduction

The dumbbell is loaded at one end. The exerciser stands erect, arms at the sides or with the free arm on the hip, and grasps the weight by the free end. He drops his wrist as far as possible and then cocks it up as high as possible. This exercises the forearm abductors: flexor carpi radialis, extensor carpi radialis, and associated muscle groups.

Wrist Adduction

The dumbbell is loaded as before but grasped so that the weight is to the back instead of forward. The movement is made through the full range of

Fig. 4.5.   Side Bend.

Fig. 4.6.   Wrist Abduction.

Photographs by Gene O'Connell

movement. This exercises the forearm adductors: flexor carpi ulnaris, extensor carpi ulnaris, and associated muscle groups.

Forearm Supination-Pronation

The exerciser sits with one forearm on his knee as for wrist curls, the hand holding a dumbbell. The forearm is rotated from full supination to full pronation. This works the forearm supinators and pronators: biceps, supinator, pronator quadratus, and associated muscle groups. A variation is to grip the free end of a dumbbell loaded at the other and to supinate and pronate the forearm.

Zottman Curl

The exerciser either stands erect or bends over at the waist, with a dumbbell held between the legs and the free hand on the knee. He curls the weight, pronates the forearm, and lowers the weight to the starting point. It is then reverse curled to the chest, the forearm is supinated, and the weight is lowered again. The amount of weight that can be handled in this exercise will, of course, be controlled by the degree of strength which can be exerted in the reverse curl. This is an excellent exercise for the elbow flexors and the forearm supinators and pronators: biceps, brachialis, brachioradialis, supinator, pronator quadratus, and associated muscle groups.

Photographs by Gene O'Connell

Fig. .4.7.   Steps in the Zottman Curl.

Triceps Extension on Bench with Dumbbells

This exercise will be recognized as a variation on the standard method of using a barbell in the standing position as described in Chapter 2. The man lies on his back on a bench, both arms fully extended upward, as though

Photographs by Gene O'Connell

Fig. 4.8.   Triceps Extension on Bench with Dumbbells.

completing a supine press with dumbbells. While the upper arms are kept elevated, the elbows are flexed and then extended. Like the barbell exercise, the effect is largely on the elbow extensors: the triceps.

Dumbbell High Pull-Up.

The exerciser assumes a lunge position, with the dumbbell close to the forward foot. He pulls it as nearly as possible straight up, ending in a position somewhat similar to that of a high pull-up. Care must be taken that the hand is not turned over and the weight pressed into the final position. This is an excellent exercise for the arm flexors and upper shoulder muscles: biceps, brachialis, brachioradialis, deltoids, supraspinatus, trapezius, and associated muscle groups.

Photographs by Gene Mozee

Fig. 4.9.   Steps in Dumbbell High Pull-Up.

CONCENTRATION EXERCISES

The basic idea underlying concentration exercises is to employ a movement which insofar as possible is restricted to the use of a given muscle group, to stabilize the joint so that accessory muscle movement is eliminated, and then to focus one's full concentration on the muscle group being exercised. How important the concentration factor is we do not know. Generally such exercises are done with a dumbbell as it is difficult to secure the required stabilization when using a barbell. Figure 4.10 shows the triceps extension exercise done as a concentration exercise. The reader will observe that the free hand is used to firmly anchor the weight-bearing arm alongside the ear, thus ensuring that the exercise is done without aid from accessory muscles or body movement. Having nothing to think of except relaxing and contracting the triceps, the exerciser is free to devote his undivided attention to this one muscle.

Photographs by Gene Mozee

Fig. 4.10.   Concentration Triceps Extension Exercise.

Concentration Curl

Perhaps the most common exercise of this type is the concentration curl. The man sits with the elbow firmly braced against the leg, as shown in figure 4.11. It is kept in this position during the entire movement. A variation is to stand behind an incline board, with the upper arm and elbow resting on the board. The forearm is extended until the arm is straight. The elbow is then flexed again without permitting the upper arm and the elbow to lose contact with the board. This is known as the **preacher curl.**

Another technique is to lie prone on a bench with the arms hanging down over the edge of the bench and to do curls while the edge of the bench prevents any backward movement of the arms. This is frequently shown in magazine articles, but is attended by difficulties in performance. Unless the bench is comparatively high off the floor, it will not be possible to extend the elbows fully. The average bench is designed primarily for bench presses and is too narrow for this sort of curling. Finally, the edge of the bench cuts into the triceps and is extremely uncomfortable.

Fig. 4.11.   Concentration Curl.

Photograph by Gene Mozee

The Concentration Dumbbell Rowing Motion

This exercise is shown in figure 4.12. Actually, the body is not too well braced in this position, and some care is required to make sure that the movement is not assisted by rotation of the torso.

There are, of course, other concentration exercises, but all work on the same principle, that is, of isolating the action of a muscle or a muscle group to as complete an extent as is possible.

Photographs by Gene Mozee

Fig. 4.12.   Concentration Dumbbell Rowing Motion.

SWING BELL

A swing bell is simply a dumbbell with the plates moved to the center so that the ends are left free for use as handles. As a result it must be used like a barbell rather than like a dumbbell. A typical swing bell exercise, the **front raise**, is shown in figure 4.13. In the writer's opinion these are awkward to use and have no particular advantages over dumbbells and barbells other than to introduce a bit of variety into the training program.

Fig. 4.13. Front Raise with Swing Bell.

IRON BOOT

The iron boot is simply a device for attaching a dumbbell to the feet. The most common exercises performed with it are the following:

1. Standing—knee flexion, straight-leg raise in front, in back and to the side.
2. Sitting—knee extension
3. Supine lying—leg raise with knee straight, leg spread, inverted bicycle ride
4. Prone lying—knee flexion
5. Side lying—leg raising

On taking measurements

5

Weight trainers are quite likely to talk of the value of exercise for health and physical fitness but to be interested primarily in the girth of their muscles. There is probably no type of recording in the entire field of physical activity so subject to exaggeration, not to say downright mendacity, as the physical measurements of body builders. He who believes everything he hears and reads about the measurements of physique competitors is credulous indeed. One should look with great suspicion upon the alleged measurements of any contestant who is not willing to have them taken by competent anthropometrists. It is strange indeed that the Mr. America anthropometric data have been permitted to rest upon nothing better than the word of the men concerned—some of whom have proved uncooperative—whereas a lifter is required to use weights checked and certified by competent weighers using tested scales.

There are standard techniques for taking anthropometric measurements, and they must be followed exactly by anyone not deliberately desiring to deceive himself and others. It is necessary that all measuring be done by a second person as it is almost impossible for a man to measure himself and be sure that the tape does not slant up, down, or sideways. Measurements must be taken BEFORE, not AFTER, exercise. The data desired are the normal sizes, not the temporary girths of muscles swollen by vigorous activity. A flexible steel tape should be used, preferably one marked off in tenths of an inch rather than in the usual sixteenths. The tape is laid on the skin and pulled snug but not tight. If too loose, it will give figures which are too large; if pulled so tightly as to cut into the flesh, it

After consulting the text for measurement techniques, chart your dimensions on the Willoughby Symmetrometer. From time to time, remeasure for changes. Is your weight training resulting in a good balance in body proportions?

will give readings which are too small. Be certain that no fingers are under the tape. This warning may seem ludicrous, but it is not an unusual situation when the circumference of the chest is being determined. Actually both sides of the body should be measured and reported, but it is the general custom to give only one figure—which, of course, may be assumed to be the one more favorable to the individual in question. Height must be taken barefoot and weight in the nude.

There is no such thing as an "official" set of prescribed measurements, but most of the recommendations made by Willoughby[1] about thirty years ago have been generally accepted and comprise the present practice. Instructions for the measurements ordinarily reported in male physique contests are as follows:

Neck—The head is erect, eyes looking forward, neck muscles relaxed. The measurement is made at the smallest girth, just above the Adam's apple.

Upper arm—The arm is raised to shoulder height and the elbow flexors are fully contracted, palm down, fist clenched and turned down. The girth is taken at the point of greatest size of the biceps. The tape must be at right angles to the upper arm bone (humerus).

Forearm—The arm is straight, with no bend at the wrist, and held at an angle away from the body. The fist is clenched so that the forearm muscles are fully contracted. The taping is made below the elbow at the point of greatest girth.

Wrist—The palm is held up, fingers extended in line with the forearm. The measurement is made at the point between the base of the hand and the bony protuberance on the little finger side of the hand (styloid process of the ulna).

Chest normal—The body is erect, the head up, breathing normal. The circumference is taken at the largest part. The tape is placed just above the nipples in front and must be straight across the back. The measurer must check carefully to make sure that the subject is not contracting the latissimus dorsi.

Chest expanded—The tape is kept in the same position as for Chest Normal while the subject inhales deeply and expands his chest to its greatest size. Again, care must be taken to see that he does not flex the latissimus dorsi in the process. One occasionally sees advertisements claiming that someone has a chest expansion of ten inches or so and can develop the same amount in those who take his course. Expansions of this kind are not typical of the experienced weight trainer. If the expanded chest measurement of such an individual exceeds the normal chest measurement by more than two or three inches, it must be carefully rechecked as the tape has probably slipped or muscle contraction has been included. Neither is there the slightest evidence that increasing the chest expansion in this manner will double one's life expectancy, as is often claimed.

Waist—The body is erect, the abdominal muscles in a normal state of tonus. The waist is measured at the smallest part, usually a little above the navel. The abdomen must not be sucked in, although figures are often cited which suggest very strongly that this is exactly what has occurred.

Thigh—The body is erect, feet about six inches apart, weight equally distributed on each foot, and thigh muscles relaxed. Measurement is made at the largest part, usually just below the buttocks.

Calf—The body is erect, with heels on the floor, the weight equally distributed on each foot. The measurement is taken at the largest girth.

Ankle—The body is erect, with the heels on the floor and the weight equally distributed on each foot. Measurement is made at the smallest part, usually about two inches above the ankle bones (lateral and medial malleolus).

In the present craze for sheer bulk, body builders frequently lose sight of the fact that the individual measurements must be in proportion if the result is to be harmonious, that is, the potential physique contest winner must be not only well developed, but also symmetrical in appearance. For some reason they have concentrated on the image of huge arms. The results have often resulted in a disproportionate body development. More losers in physique contests suffer from the fact that their legs seem underdeveloped in comparison with their arms and upper body than from the other way around.

What is the average American male physique and what sort of development must he attain if he is to have a chance to win in topnotch competition? A wealth of data has been collected in the last few years by anthropologists for the Army Quartermaster Corps, equipment manufacturers, space travel scientists, and others, but for the most part it is much more concerned with lengths than with girths. The figures in Table 5.1 date back to the 1940s and are quite incomplete, but are probably reasonably descriptive of the average young American male of today.

How such an individual appears can be seen in figure 5.1, which is a photograph of the statue of "Norman" created by a sculptor working under

Table 5.1.   Anthropometry of the Average American Male

Height	68.5 in.
Weight	140-150 lbs.
Upper arm	10 in.
Chest normal	34 in.
Waist	30 in.
Thigh	20 in.
Calf	14 in.

the direction of Dr. Robert L. Dickson to depict the average American of that time. Norman's physique may be compared with that of the "ideal" as represented by the various Mr. Americas. The anthropometric data for the winners to date are given in Table 5.2, and a photograph of one of them, Bill Pearl, is reproduced in figure 5.2 for comparison with Norman. The contrast is startling, to say the least.

The authentic Mr. America contest is sponsored by the Amateur Athletic Union (AAU) and is held in conjunction with the Senior National

Photograph courtesy of American Museum of Natural History

Fig. 5.1.   Norman, the Average American Male of a Few Years Ago.

Photograph courtesy of Pearl & Stern

Fig. 5.2.   William Pearl, Mr. America 1953, Mr. Universe 1953, Professional Mr. Universe 1961 and 1967, who represents a present-day American male ideal.

Table 5.2. Anthropometric Measurements of the AAU Mr. Americas 1940-1974

Year		Height	Weight	Neck	Chest, normal	Chest, ex-panded	Arm	Forearm	Wrist	Waist	Thigh	Calf	Ankle
1940-41	John C. Grimek	5'8.50"	195	18.00	49.70	50.70	18.70	14.50	7.70	31.00	27.00	17.70	10.00
1942	Frank Leight	5'11.25"	209	17.00	46.90	49.50	17.00	15.00	7.95	32.00	25.00	15.00	10.25
1943	Jules Bacon	5'7"	178	16.50	46.10		16.60	12.70	7.00	29.90	25.00	15.70	8.60
1944	Steve Stanko	5'11.50"	203	17.50	48.50	50.00	18.50	13.40	7.95	30.00	28.00	16.75	10.00
1945	Clarence Ross	5'9.50"	190	16.75	47.25		17.30	13.50	7.50	32.00	25.30	16.10	9.00
1946	Alan Stephan	5'11.50"	205	17.50	48.50	50.25	18.10	14.50	7.50	31.50	26.00	17.00	10.50
1947	Steve Reeves	6'1"	213	17.50	49.50	51.00	18.00		7.50	29.00	25.50	17.75	9.30
1948	George Eiferman	5'8"	200	17.25	47.50	50.00	18.00	13.25	7.25	32.00	24.50	16.00	9.75
1949	Jack Delinger	5'8"	205	18.00	50.00	52.00	19.00	14.25	8.00	31.00	26.50	17.25	10.00
1950	John Farbotnik	5'9"	195	17.00	50.00	51.00	18.00		7.25	32.00	25.50	16.25	
1951	Roy S. Hilligenn	5'6"	178	17.50	48.50		17.75	14.50	7.50	31.00	24.50	16.25	8.00
1952	James Park	5'9"	187		49.00		18.60			30.00	28.00	17.00	
1953	William Pearl	5'11.25"	193	17.62	48.25	50.00	18.00	15.00	7.25	32.50	24.50	16.75	9.50
1954	Richard DuBois	6'1"	225	18.00	50.00	52.00	18.50	15.00	8.00	32.25	26.50	17.00	
1955	Steve D. Klisanin	5'10"	185	17.00	47.00	49.00	18.00	14.50	7.75	31.00	25.00	17.00	11.00
1956	Ray Schaefer	5'10"	202										
1957	Ronald Lacy	5'9"	185	17.00	47.00	49.50	17.00	13.50	7.25	30.00	24.50	17.00	9.10
1958	Tom Sansone*	5'11"	212	17.50	50.00	52.00	19.25	15.50	7.75	31.50	26.00	17.50	10.00
1959	Harry Johnson	5'8.75"	185	16.75	45.00	47.50	16.90	13.00	7.75	30.00	24.00	16.00	9.25
1960	Lloyd Lerille	5'6"	180	16.75	47.50	50.50	17.12	13.25	8.00	31.00	24.00	16.25	9.00
1961	Ray Routledge	6'	200	17.50	50.00	51.00	18.50	16.00	8.00	32.00	26.50	17.50	9.50
1962	Joe Abbenda	6'	205	17.50	49.50	51.00	18.25	14.75	7.25	32.00	25.50	16.25	9.00
1963	Vern Weaver	5'9.50"	205	17.50	49.50	51.00	18.75	13.50	7.75	32.00	26.00	17.25	9.50
1964	Val Vasilieff	5'11"	210	18.00	52.00	54.00	19.00	16.50	8.35	30.00	27.00	18.00	10.00
1965	Jerry Daniels	6'0.25"	224	18.00	49.25	51.00	18.75	14.50	7.50	32.50	26.50	17.00	10.50
1966	Bob Gajda	5'9.50"	200	19.00	47.00	48.50	18.50	14.50	7.50	28.00	25.00	18.50	10.75
1967	Dennis Tinerino	6'1"	220	18.00	50.00	53.00	19.50	15.00	7.50	33.00	27.00	18.00	10.50
1968	James Haislop	5'11.50"	222	18.00	50.00	51.50	19.00	14.50	7.25	31.00	27.50	18.25	9.50
1969	Boyer Coe	5'8"	210										
1970	Chris Dickerson	5'6"	188	17.50	47.50	49.50	18.00	14.00	7.75	32.00	25.25	18.00	9.50
1971	Casey Viator	5'8"	217		50.00		19.36			31.50	28.00	18.00	
1972	Steve Michelik	5'10"	215		50.00		19.00			28.00	27.00	18.00	
1973	James Morris	5'11"	221	17.50	49.00	50.50	19.25	17.00	7.75	32.00	25.50	17.00	9.50
1974	Ron Thompson		210										

*Deceased 1975

Note: Physical measurements of body builders are often exaggerated. Most of these data were obtained from the Mr. Americas themselves, but accuracy cannot be guaranteed. Some proved uncooperative, and their data are either missing or obtained from other sources.

Weight Lifting Championships. Judges are appointed by the National AAU Weight Lifting Chairman and the following scoring table is used:

Table 5.3.   Scoring for Mr. America Contest

Category	Points
Symmetry	25
Muscularity	25
Presentation	25
Interview	5

It will be noted that there is no requirement that the contestants demonstrate an ability to use their muscles. At the time of the inception of these contests, the competitors were largely weight lifters, and Mr. Americas like John Grimek and Steve Stanko were champion lifters as well as physique competition winners. As time went on, it became evident that the type of body build which wins the physique contests is markedly different from that typical of the champion weight lifters. The physique winner tends to have comparatively small bones, joints, waist, hips, and buttocks, combined with broad shoulders and a huge chest (fig. 5.3). The lifter is likely to have comparatively big bones, a relatively long trunk, short arms and legs, a thick waist, and well-developed buttocks (fig. 5.4).

Some of the earlier Mr. Americas like Grimek (fig. 5.6) were champion lifters, and some have been outstanding athletes (fig. 5.5), but the trend has been steadily away from performance and toward display. At the present time champion weight lifters do not win Mr. America contests, and Mr. Americas do not win weight-lifting championships.

A further word of explanation about the Mr. America title might clarify the picture for the newcomer to the field of weight training. Apparently the title is not copyrighted, and the idea of using it occurred independently to two entrepreneurs in 1939. In connection with the AAU weight-lifting championships in Chicago that year a board of artists and other aesthetes selected the handsome but underdeveloped Roland Essmaker as Mr. America. That same year Bert Goodrich, a worthy choice, was awarded the same title in an Amsterdam, New York, contest. In 1940 competition was held on a truly national basis and was won by John C. Grimek. When he repeated his triumph the following year and appeared likely to continue to do so indefinitely, a rule was passed prohibiting a winner from competing in future contests. The men officially recognized as titleholders by the Amateur Athletic Union are listed in Table 5.2.

As interest in the event increased, some of the professional wrestlers took to calling themselves Mr. America, although they had no legitimate claim to this designation. Eventually, ambitious promoters organized rival

Fig. 5.3   **Fig. 5.4**   **Fig. 5.5**

Fig. 5.3. Steve Reeves, 1947 Mr. America. Many fans still consider Reeves to have been the greatest example of the **V** shape in the history of physique contests. (Courtesy **Iron Man Magazine.**)

Fig. 5.4. Vasily Alexeev (USSR), 1972 Olympic Superheavyweight Weight Lifting Champion. This great lifter exemplifies the barrellike physique characteristics of the giants of strength. He is 6'1" tall and weighs 330 lbs. Alexeev holds sixty-nine world's weight lifting records. (Courtesy **Iron Man Magazine.**)

Fig. 5.5. Ronald Lacy, Mr. America and Most Muscular 1957. Lacy attended college on a football scholarship and earned letters in three sports.

Fig. 5.6. John C. Grimek, Mr. America 1940-41, Mr. USA 1948, Mr. Universe, and considered by many authorities to possess the most perfect male physique of all time, is a former National and North American Weight Lifting Champion. He was a member of the 1936 Olympic team and represented the United States in the World Weight Lifting Championships in 1938. This athlete competed in both the light heavyweight and the heavyweight divisions. He has held various national records. His left-hand clean and jerk as a heavyweight still stands.

Fig. 5.6

groups such as the International Federation of Body Builders (IFBB) and the World Body Building Guild, awarded this same title to the winners, and began publicizing them accordingly in their magazines. This has been the source of a great deal of confusion. The men listed in Table 5.2 are the only ones recognized by the AAU as authorized to use this title. They should not be confused with the winners of the Mr. USA title, competition for which is held in conjunction with the Senior National Power Lifting Championships. Quite often a competitor has won both titles.

Probably the most prestige is attached to the winning of one of the shows produced in London by the National Amateur Body Builders Association (NABBA), the largest organization of its kind. In spite of its name the NABBA does not have the backing of any amateur association. Originally both amateurs and professionals competed against each other, but in 1952 separate classes for each were introduced. It has been declared an outlaw by the international amateur body, The Federation International Halterophile et Culturiste. Whether amateur standing is of any particular value to a physique contestant who has little or no interest in entering weight-lifting meets or other amateur athletic events is questionable. The NABBA and the IFBB have continued to attract a sizeable array of famed body builders. The picture is further confused by the fact that the British Weight Lifting Association, the IFBB, and other promoters have sponsored shows at which they awarded the title Mr. Universe to the winner. The situation is analogous to that in professional wrestling where a man may be a "World Champion" on his own circuit and almost completely unknown elsewhere.

It is, of course, totally unrealistic for the average man to hope to attain the measurements claimed by the Mr. Americas. A much more rational approach is for him to set as his goal attainment of a physique which is both well developed and well balanced, even if not as massive as that of physique contest winners. On the basis of over fifty years of observation and study of well-developed athletes and body builders, the noted anthropometrist and historian of weight training David P. Willoughby has devised a chart on which an individual can plot his measurements and determine the symmetry of his body. With this information available, he can determine at a glance what parts require specialized training and evaluate the results of such training over short or long periods of time. Table 5.4 is a considerably abridged form of the Willoughby Chart.

REFERENCES

1. David P. Willoughby. *How to Take Your Measurements*. (Montreal: Your Physique Publishing Co., 1944).
2. *Official AAU Weightlifting Rule Book*. (Indianapolis: Amateur Athletic Union of the United States, 1974).

Table 5.4. Willoughby Symmetrometer

Status of Ratio or Measurement — Weight ÷ Height →	Minimum		Small					Medium				Large						Maximum			
	1.6	1.7	1.8	1.9	2.0	2.1	2.2	2.3	2.4	2.5	2.6	2.7	2.8	2.9	3.0	3.1	3.2	3.3	3.4	3.5	3.6
Neck	13.0			14.0			15.0			16.0			17.0			18.0			19.0		
Biceps, R.	12.1		13.0			14.0			15.0			16.0			17.0			18.0			
** ,, L.**	12.0			13.0			14.0			15.0			16.0			17.0			18.0		
Forearm, R.	10.1			11.0			12.0				13.0				14.0				15.0		
** ,, L.**	10.0			11.0				12.0			13.0				14.0				15.0		
Wrist, R.					6.5							7.5				8.0			8.5		
** ,, L.**			6.0					7.0							8.0						
Chest (normal)		34.0	35.0	36.0	37.0	38.0	39.0	40.0	41.0	42.0	43.0	44.0	45.0	46.0	47.0		48.0	49.0			50.0
Waist	25.0	26.0	27.0		28.0	29.0		30.0	31.0	32.0		33.0	34.0		35.0		36.0		37.0		38.0
Hips	30.0	31.0	32.0	33.0		34.0	35.0	36.0	37.0	38.0		39.0	40.0		41.0	42.0		43.0	44.0	45.0	46.0
Thigh, R.	18.0		19.0		20.0	21.0		22.0		23.0		24.0			25.0		26.0		27.0		
** ,, L.**	18.0		19.0		20.0	21.0		22.0		23.0		24.0			25.0		26.0		27.0		
Knee, R.	12.0			13.0			14.0			15.0			16.0			17.0			18.0		
** ,, L.**	12.0			13.0			14.0			15.0			16.0			17.0			18.0		
Calf, R.	12.0		13.0			14.0				15.0		16.0				17.0			18.0		
** ,, L.**	12.0		13.0			14.0				15.0		16.0				17.0			18.0		
Ankle, R.	7.0		7.5		8.0			8.5		9.0				9.5		10.0			10.5		
** ,, L.**	7.0		7.5		8.0			8.5		9.0				9.5		10.0			10.5		

Girths (row group label for Neck through Ankle)

Instructions: Make the required measurements according to the directions given earlier in chapter 5 and plot the data on the appropriate scales by making heavy dots at the proper points. Plot the larger of the two arms as the right arm, regardless of whether it is actually the right or the left, and vice versa. Connect the dots by means of a heavy line. The more nearly this coincides with a line drawn perpendicularly from the Weight/Height point to the bottom of the chart, the more symmetrical are the proportions of the body. A variation of ±2.5 percent is acceptable. To help in visualizing these limits, parallel lines may be drawn at 1.05 and 0.95 percent of the Weight/Height figure. In obese individuals body weight will take care of itself if the oversized areas, particularly the waist, are brought into line with the other girth measurements, particularly the wrists and ankles. (Copyright by David P. Willoughby. Reproduced by special permission.)

Weight
training for athletes

6

The key question in any discussion of the development of muscles is, What can you do with them? Harry B. Paschall's famous cartoon character Bosco used to present the moment of truth to the body builders with his "Vell, ve roll oudt de veights und ve see vhat you can lift." Yet there are few questions in the field of physical training which are more controversial than the relationship between increases in strength and gains in performance. For every thesis or published study reporting that the practice of progressive resistance exercises improved performance in swimming, running, jumping, or some other activity there is another stating that no such benefits could be observed. Pierson and Rasch were forced to conclude:

> The role of strength in motor performance is not clear, the effect of strength development in conditioning to the rigors of an activity is conjectural, and the evidence concerning the relationships of strength, body size, and composition is contradictory.[1]

Obviously a certain amount of strength is necessary for successful participation in any sport. Once this level is reached, further gains in strength do not appear to be accompanied by equivalent increases in performance. The optimal strength levels for various forms of activity are not known, however, and it is probably safe to assume that most athletes will profit by developing more than they have. The training programs which follow have been selected with a view to showing what is actually being done in certain fields of athletics today. They will serve to give the reader some idea of what those closely connected with these sports believe best meet their needs, but

---

Analyze your favorite sport in terms of the muscle groups subjected to the greatest stress. Devise a weight-training program designed to meet these particular needs.

---

they should not be blindly accepted nor assumed to constitute some sort of an argument against personal experimentation.

Of all the professional developers of competitive athletes the football coaches seem to have been the most progressive in incorporating weight training into their conditioning programs. So far as the writer has been able to determine, the most comprehensive procedure of this type is that employed by the University of Texas. It is considerably more elaborate than it is practical to present here, but the following description will at least give a good idea of its major facets.

Like many other coaches, the Longhorns are partial to circuit training because of the cardiorespiratory benefits believed to result from its use. The circuit used by them during the end of the football season and the beginning of spring practice includes the following stations: (1) standing press; (2) upright rowing motion; (3) squat jump (maximum number in 15 seconds); (4) bent-over rowing motion; (5) bench press; (6) stair climb, using two 20-inch steps (maximum number in 1 minute); (7) parallel bar dip (maximum number); (8) barbell curl; (9) dead lift and shoulder shrug; (10) sit-ups on incline board (maximum number in 25 seconds with board at a 30-degree angle); (1) knee extension-flexion.

The athlete is tested to determine the maximum load with which he can accomplish three repetitions of each of the barbell exercises. He is then assigned weights 20 to 30 percent of this figure and timed to determine how long it takes him to complete three laps around the circuit without any rest pauses between stations or laps. Next he is assigned a target time about one-third less than this figure. When he can complete the circuit in the target time, the work load is increased, the man is retested, and a new target time is established (fig. 6.1).

Between the end of spring training and the beginning of the summer vacation the players are placed on a regular barbell program stressing the development of strength. The schedule includes the following exercises: (1) standing press, (2) curl, (3) bent-over rowing, (4) upright rowing, (5) dead lift, (6) shoulder shrug, (7) bench press, (8) half-squat, (9) heel raise, (10) squat run—40 pounds for 8 seconds.

All exercises are performed for two sets, but the number of repetitions differs according to the position played.

A somewhat similar training program plus some isometric exercises and quarter-mile runs is followed during the summer vacation.[2]

For many schools and colleges such a program would be too elaborate to be practical. They might prefer the more conventional program followed by Louisiana State University:

Exercise	Sets	Repetitions
Clean and press	4	6
Pull-up to waist	4	4
Squat	4	8
Bench press	4	8
Dead lifts	4	6

Kloppenburg[3] prefers the variable resistance apparatus shown in figure 3.9 (p. 45) and has his players perform two sets of the following exercises three times each week, emphasizing the use of weights which require an all-out effort:

Exercise	Repetitions
Bench press	5
Heel raise	12
Leg press	12
Standing press	5
Latissimus machine	5
Triceps extension	5
Cleans	5
Curls	5
Reverse curls	5

Photograph courtesy of Burnham

Fig. 6.1. University of Texas Football Players Training with the Weights. The man on the right is Tommy Nobis, All-American and All-Professional guard.

Perhaps the program which has received the greatest acceptance among baseball players is that presented by Wickstrom.[4] The exercises, with the proposed starting weights for each, follow:

(1) clean and press—one-third body weight plus 10 pounds, (2) straight-arm pull-overs—one-quarter body weight minus 5 pounds, (3) sit-ups—with hands behind the head and no weight, (4) supine press—one-half body weight (5) bent-over lateral raise—10 to 15 pounds dumbbells, (6) half-squats—one-half body weight, (7) ulnar flexion of wrist—5 pounds, and (8) wrist curl—35 pounds.

Wickstrom suggests two or three sets of five to seven repetitions each, with three to five minutes of rest between each set. He believes that this schedule should be used three times a week for off-season or preseason conditioning.

Edwards[5] has worked out a set of movements specific for baseball. They include: (1) trunk rotation—arms held out to the sides on line with the shoulders, a six-to-ten-pound dumbbell in each hand; body twisted as far as possible to one side and then to the other; (2) one-hand swing—an eight-or-ten-pound dumbbell held at the opposite shoulder and swung across the chest as if batting; (3) wrist curls—done standing with the forearms parallel to the ground; (4) triceps extension; (5) wrist abductor.

In spite of the fact that it was originally published several years ago, the O'Connor and Sills[6] program seems to have retained favor among basketball players. They especially recommend it for preseason training, although suggesting that it may be continued during the season: (1) wrist curls, (2) curls, (3) side raises with dumbbells, (4) presses, (5) forward raise with dumbbells, (6) heel raise, (7) walking squats with barbell on shoulders.

They propose ten to twelve repetitions of each arm exercise and two sets of ten to twelve repetitions for the legs.

Burnham[7] offers a training schedule especially designed to develop rebounding ability: (1) Military press, (2) erect rowing, (3) bent rowing, (4) two-arm curl, (5) running in place with twenty-pound jacket in half-squat position, (6) stair step, (7) heel raise.

The barbell exercises are to be done in three sets of eight to twelve repetitions each. Running in place is performed for five sets of ten seconds each.

The weight-training program prescribed by Higgins[8] for the swimmers at the United States Naval Academy consists of the following: (1) pull-up to chest, (2) press, (3) press off the back of the neck, (4) push-out—weight is held at the chest and pushed out horizontally to full arm extension, (5) hold-out—weight is pushed out from the chest, held in that position as long as possible, and returned to the chest when it is ready to drop, (6) back push-outs—weight is held behind the body and pushed back as far as possible without bending the arms (some men will find that this produces severe cramps or cramping pains in the triceps), (7) squats (especially recommended for backstrokers), (8) straight-arm pull-overs on the floor—weight moves in an arc from overhead to the thighs and back.

Higgins says that the point of these exercises is to develop strength, not bulk, as the latter is undesirable for a swimmer. His men start out with about 38 to 40 pounds and 25 repetitions and work up to 75 repetitions without increasing the weights. His team normally employs this program four days a week, but discontinues it two days before meets in which especially severe competition is anticipated. It might be mentioned that this is consistent with the theory that about two days layoff from heavy work is required to permit the carbohydrate stores in the liver and muscle to fill prior to events which require a maximal expenditure of energy.

Track and field events are so varied that it is difficult to prescribe a general program that will meet the needs of competitors in each event. Berger,[9] however, offers the following off-season program: (1) curl, (2) bench press, (3) one-third squat, (4) upright rowing, (5) sit-up, (6) leg curl with iron boot, (7) forward bend with barbell behind neck, (8) heel raise, (9) press, (10) side bend with barbell on shoulders, (11) wrist curl, (12) knee extension in seated position.

He does not recommend this for use during the season as he believes that the fatigue which results from its practice may distract from the development of sports skills.

Weight training is especially popular among the weight throwers. Gary Gubner in effect had a choice of participating in the 1964 Olympic Games as a shot-putter or as a weight lifter. The following program is used by Jay Silvester, the best combined shot-put and discus thrower in the world: (1) clean and jerk, (2) dead lift, (3) bench press, (4) jumping squats, (5) lateral raises on an incline board, (6) triceps extension, (7) press on an incline board, (8) sit-ups.

His program is of the light and heavy variety. He lifts three days a week during the off-season and two or three days a week during the competitive season, depending upon how he feels.[10]

John P. Jesse, who has had considerable success working with weight throwers and other athletes in Southern California, believes that training programs for the former should stress the development of power in the hamstrings, lower back, abdomen, serratus anterior, hands, and fingers. In his opinion too many weight throwers make the mistake of attempting to gain tremendous overall strength while actually neglecting the muscles most important for success in their particular sport.

The physical appearance of the actors commonly seen in the televised "displays of wrestling skills" have accustomed their audiences to think of wrestlers as men of tremendous physical development or as fat men. This type of build, however, is not characteristic of the nonprofessional. Top-flight amateur wrestlers tend to be very similar in body structure to sprinters. Both are likely to be relatively short, due to their short legs, but the wrestlers have larger arms in relation to their calves and thighs than do the track athletes. Strength tests of American and Japanese wrestlers indicated that these men, at least, were not particularly strong.[11]

Unlike the football coaches, wrestling experts have tended to be more or less skeptical of the benefits of weight training for the amateur grappler. However, Bill Farwell, coach of the highly successful 1972 United States Olympic Wrestling Team, considers that his emphasis on weight training was one of the principal reasons why his team was so outstanding. He employed an earlier version of the machine shown in figure 3.9 (p. 45). The wrestlers performed three circuits three days a week, working at 75 to 80 percent of maximum. He suggests that this program be performed only twice a week during the wrestling season, preferably at least two to three hours before practice.[12]

Teams which do not have this particular piece of apparatus available might well use a conventional standard double progressive system introduced to the United States Coast Guard Academy by Kapral.[13] The exercises include: (1) standing press, (2) sit-ups with bent knees, (3) curls in strict style, (4) straight-arm pull-overs on mat, (5) squats, (6) standing lateral raise with dumbbells, (7) bench press, (8) upright rowing motion, (9) straight-legged dead lift, (10) bent-arm lateral raise on bench, (11) wrist curls, (12) bent-over rowing motion.

This program would be improved by the addition of neck exercises and trunk-twisting exercises of various kinds since powerful rotational movements of the torso are an integral part of a great percentage of wrestling moves. Figure 6.2 shows an individual who has been unusually successful both in wrestling and in body building.

Fig. 6.2. Lloyd "Red" Lerille, Mr. America 1960. Lerille was undefeated during three seasons of high school wrestling and was runner-up in the All-Navy championships before deciding to devote his full attention to body building.

The following program is used by students of judo who attend the Kodokan.[14] It is of particular interest because of its stress on the use of dumbbells. Perhaps this has resulted from the fact that Japanese studies have shown that the top judoka were lacking in back and arm strength. The exercises include: (1) squat, (2) dumbbell straight-arm pull-over (3) heel raise, (4) dumbbell press on bench, (5) flying motion, (6) dumbbell rowing, (7) barbell curl, (8) standing barbell triceps extension, (9) seated dumbbell press behind neck, (10) sit-ups.

A number of alternate programs are presented by Ishikawa and Draeger.[15] These experts recommend that a schedule of three sets of ten repetitions each be followed.

Fig. 6.3.   Val Vasilieff, Mr. America 1964, in a relaxed pose rather than in a tensed pose, as usually assumed by physique contestants. Willoughby (in **The Super Athletes,** p. 167) credits Vasilieff with a correct two-hands curl of 220 pounds, a press of 315 pounds, a snatch of 270 pounds, a clean and jerk of 360 pounds, a bench press of 450 pounds, and a two-hands dead lift of 600 pounds—rather convincing evidence that shapeliness and strength may be combined.

The reader who desires a more detailed discussion of weight training for athletes than is possible in these pages is referred to the more detailed discussions in such specialized texts as those by Jesse.[16, 17, 18] The point to be remembered is that the more closely a weight-training movement simulates an actual movement of the sport, the more helpful it is likely to be. A typical example might be the use of a dumbbell with the weight at one end (p. 51) as the basis for a series of exercises for tennis. The reader can design his own program by determining which muscles are the most important in a given sport and then using the Muscle Chart as a guide to effective exercises for those muscles.

REFERENCES

1. William R. Pierson, and Philip J. Rasch. "Strength Development and Performance Capacity." *Journal of the Association for Physical and Mental Rehabilitation* 17:5 *et seq.*, January-February 1963.
2. Terry Todd. "Progressive Resistance for Football at the University of Texas." *Strength & Health* 32:18 *et seq.*, September, 1964.
3. Bob Kloppenberg. "Conditioning for Football." *Athletic Journal* 54:44 *et seq.*, February 1974.
4. Ralph L. Wickstrom. "Weight Training for Baseball." *Scholastic Coach* 29:36 *et seq.*, March 1960.
5. Donald K. Edwards. "A Strength Building Program for Baseball," *Athletic Journal* 45:12 *et seq.* (February 1965).
6. Frank "Bucky" O'Connor, and Frank Sills. "Heavy Resistance Exercises for Basketball Players," *Athletic Journal*, 36:6-8 (June 1956).
7. Stan Burnham. "Develop Your Rebounders with Weight Training," *Scholastic Coach* (30 December 1960).
8. John H. Higgins. "Success with the Weights," *Swimming World* 2:4 *et seq.* (October 1961).
9. Richard A. Berger. "Strength Training for Track and Field," *Athletic Journal* 43:50 *et seq.* (February 1963).
10. Dale O. Nelson. "Strength Training with Jay Silvester," *All American Athlete* 6:10 *et seq.* (July 1964).
11. Philip J. Rasch *et al.* "Effect of Training for Amateur Wrestling on Total Proportional Strength Scores." *Research Quarterly* 32:201-207 (May 1961).
12. W. Farrell. Personal communication, 1 April 1974.
13. Frank S. Kapral. *Coach's Illustrated Guide to Championship Wrestling* (Englewood Cliffs, N. J.: Prentice-Hall, Inc., 1964).
14. Donn Draeger. "Weight Lifting for Judo," *Strength & Health*, June 1960.
15. Takahiko Ishikawa, and Donn E. Draeger, *Judo Training Methods: A Sourcebook* (Rutland, Vt.: Charles E. Tuttle Co., Inc., 1962), pp. 130-137.
16. John Jesse. *Explosive Muscular Power for Championship Football* (Pasadena, Calif.: Athletic Press, 1968).
17. John Jesse. *Strength, Power and Muscular Endurance for Runners and Hurdlers* (Pasadena, Calif.: Athletic Press, 1971).
18. John Jesse. *Wrestling Physical Conditioning Encyclopedia* (Pasadena, Calif.: Athletic Press, 1974).

Fig. 6.4. Superficial Muscles of the Human Body, Anterior View. From King, B. G., and Showers, M. J.: **Human Anatomy and Physiology.** Ed. 5. Philadelphia, W. B. Saunders Company, 1953.

Fig. 6.5. Superficial Muscles of the Human Body, Posterior View. From King, B. G., and Showers J. J.: **Human Anatomy and Physiology.** Ed. 5. Philadelphia, W. B. Saunders Company, 1953.

Selected references

The following list of suggested readings is presented for the guidance of the serious weight trainer who desires a more complete understanding of the scientific facts underlying his form of training.

Clarke, David H. "Adaptations in Strength and Muscular Endurance Resulting from Exercise." In Wilmore, Jack K., ed., *Exercise and Sport Sciences Review.* New York: Academic Press, 1973, 1:73-102.

"Development of Muscular Strength and Endurance," *Physical Fitness Research Digest,* January 1974.

Golding, Lawrence A. "Drugs and Hormones." In Morgan, William P., ed. *Ergogenic Aids and Muscular Performance.* New York: Academic Press, Inc., 1972, pp. 367-397.

"Isometric Versus Isotonic Exercises," *Physical Fitness Research Digest,* July 1971.

Karpovich, Peter V., and Sinning, Wayne E. *Physiology of Muscular Activity,* 7th ed. Philadelphia: W. B. Saunders Co., 1971.

Mueller, E. A. "The Physiological Basis of Rest Pauses in Heavy Work," *Quarterly Journal of Experimental Physiology and Cognate Medical Sciences* 38:205-215, 1952.

Muller, Erich A. Influence of Training and of Inactivity on Muscle Strength," *Archives of Physical Medicine and Rehabilitation* 51:449-462, August 1970.

"Organic Foods," Food Technology 28:71-74, January 1974.

Present Knowledge in Nutrition, 3rd ed. New York: Nutrition Foundation, Inc., 1967.

National Academy of Sciences. *Recommended Daily Allowances.* 8th revised ed. Washington, D. C., 1973.

Rasch, Philip J. "An Introduction to the History of Weight Training in the United States." In Sills, Frank, ed., *Weight Training in Sports and Physical Education*. Washington, D. C.: AAHPER, 1962, pp. 1-14.

Rasch, Philip J. "Isometric Exercise and Gains of Muscle Strength." In Shephard, Roy J., ed. *Frontiers of Fitness*. Springfield, Ill.: Charles C Thomas, 1971, pp. 98-111.

Rasch, Philip J. "The Present Status of Negative (Eccentric) Exercise: A Review." *American Corrective Therapy Journal*, May-June 1974.

Rasch, Philip J., and Burke, Roger K. *Kinesiology and Applied Anatomy*. 5th ed. Philadelphia: Lea & Febiger, 1974.

"Toward a Better Understanding of Muscular Strength," *Physical Fitness Research Digest*, January 1973.

Willoughby, David P. *The Super Athletes*. New York: A. S. Barnes and Co., Inc., 1970.

GLOSSARY OF TECHNICAL TERMS

Abduction. Movement away from the center line of the body.

Adduction. Movement toward the center line of the body.

Anabolic steroids. Synthetic hormones believed to promote growth of protein tissue.

Clean and jerk. An Olympic lift in which the weight is taken to the chest in one movement and then thrown overhead in a second movement.

Cuts. The separations seen between groups of muscle fibers in men in whom intensive training has produced a high degree of muscular definition.

Endocrine glands. Glands which secrete a substance that affects another organ or part of the body.

Hormones. Chemical substances which can alter the functional activity of an organ of the body.

Hypertrophy. Enlargement in the size of a muscle. Increases in hypertrophy are not necessarily closely related to increases in strength.

Isokinetic. Constant motion; an isotonic contraction in which the speed of movement remains steady.

Isometric. Constant length; a contraction in which there is no apparent change in the angles of the bony levers.

Isotonic. Constant tension; a contraction in which the angles between the bony levers change.

Negative exercise. A form of isotonic exercise in which the muscle lengthens rather than shortens. Also called eccentric exercise.

Power clean. An exercise in which a weight is taken from knee level to the shoulders in one movement.

Prone. Face downward. The bench press is often erroneously termed the prone press. A true prone press would be a push-up.

Snatch.   An Olympic lift in which a weight is raised overhead in a single movement.

Sticking point.   The point in a lift at which the greatest effort is required in order to complete the movement. This occurs at the joint angle at which the mechanical efficiency is least advantageous.

Supine.   Face up.

Synergistic action.   Simultaneous contraction of two or more muscles to produce a desired action.

Summary of Muscle Actions and Most Effective Exercises

Muscle	Principal Function	Most Effective Exercises
Abdominis obliquus	Flexion of trunk, flexion to same side, rotation to opposite side	Side bending while holding weight in one hand, twisting sit-ups and leg raises, body twists with barbell on shoulders
Abdominis rectus	Flexion of spine	Sit-ups, vee-ups
Biceps brachii	Flexion and inward rotation of forearm	All forms of curls, reverse curls, and supination-pronation movements
Biceps femoris	Extends thigh, flexes knee	Squats, leg press, leg curls, and leg backward raises with iron boot
Brachialis	Principal flexor of elbow	All forms of curls and reverse curls
Brachioradialis	Flexion of elbow	See Biceps brachii
Deltoid	Three-part muscle; part 1, performs horizontal flexion; part 2, abduction; part 3, horizontal extension	All overhead lifts, side and front raises
Erector spinae	Extension of trunk	Dead lifts, good morning exercise, swan exercise, side bends, dead lifts
Extensor carpi radialis	Extension and abduction of wrist	Reverse wrist curls, wrist abduction exercise
Extensor carpi ulnaris	Extension and adduction of wrist	Reverse wrist curls, wrist adduction exercise
Flexor carpi radialis	Flexion and abduction of wrist	Wrist curls, wrist abduction exercise
Flexor carpi ulnaris	Flexion and adduction of wrist	Wrist curls, wrist adduction exercise

Muscle	Principal Function	Most Effective Exercises
Gastrocnemius	Extends foot; aids in flexing knee	Heel raises, donkey raises in regular and inverted positions, walking on toes with barbell on shoulders
Gluteus maximus	Extension and outward rotation of thigh	Squat, backward leg extension with iron boot, outward rotation of leg with iron boot
Latissimus dorsi	Draws arms downward, backward, and inward	Lat machine, rowing motion, pull-over
Pectoralis major	Two-part muscle; part 1, functions in arm flexion and abduction; part 2, in arm extension and adduction	Pull-over, flying motion, bench press
Pronator quadratus	Pronates forearm	Pronation-supination of wrist
Quadriceps femoris	Extends knee	Squat, leg press, forward raise of leg, and seated knee extension with iron boot
Rectus femoris	Extends knee and flexes thigh; part of quadriceps femoris	See Quadriceps femoris
Rhomboids	Adduct scapula	Rowing motion, shoulder shrugs
Semimembranosus and semitendinosus (hamstrings)	Extends thigh and flexes knee	Squats, leg press, leg curls with iron boots, backward leg raises
Serratus anterior	Abduction of scapula	All overhead lifts, lateral raise, pull-over
Soleus	Extends foot	See Gastrocnemius
Sternocleidomastoid	Flexes and rotates head	Bridging, use of weights suspended from head strap
Supinator	Supinates forearm	Supination-pronation exercise
Supraspinatus	Arm abduction	All overhead lifts, front and side raises
Teres major	Same as latissimus dorsi	See Latissimus dorsi
Trapezius	Elevates shoulders and abducts scapula	Shoulder shrugs, all overhead lifts, dead lifts
Triceps brachii	Extension of elbow joint	Overhead lifts, bench presses, French press
Vastus intermedius, internus, and medialis	Parts of quadriceps femoris	See Quadriceps femoris

Appendix:
Questions and answers

MULTIPLE CHOICE

1. The greatest prestige is attached to winning
   a. the AAU Mr. America
   b. the IFBB Mr. America
   C. the NABBA Mr. Universe
   d. the WBBG Mr. America   (p. 64)
2. The lifters at York have popularized
   A. the heavy and light system
   b. the light and heavy system
   c. the set system   (p. 34)
3. The use of the squat with heavy weights was popularized by
   A. Mark H. Berry   b. Bob Hoffman   c. Henry J. Atkin   (p. 19)
4. In the opinion of Peary Rader, the most effective system for building up the arms is
   a. sets   b. supersets   c. super multiple sets   (p. 39)
5. The "Valsalva phenomenon" results from
   A. a sudden rise in blood pressure, followed by a sudden drop
   b. a sudden drop in blood pressure, followed by a sudden rise
   c. a sudden and sustained rise in blood pressure   (p. 28-29)
6. As a rough guide a beginner may start his presses with
   A. one quarter of his body weight   c. one half of his body weight
   b. one third of his body weight   (p. 30)
7. The amount of force that a muscle can exert depends on the number and size of its
   a. sarcoplasm   b. sarcolemma   c. myofibrils   (p. 3)
8. The PHA System is the opposite of the
   a. rest-pause system   c. multipoundage system
   B. blitz system   (p. 36)
9. The most popular piece of equipment in the average gym is
   a. the incline board   b. the calf machine   C. the lat machine   (p. 41)
10. The present trend in set training is
    a. to use lighter weights in each successive set
    B. to use the same weight in each successive set
    c. to use heavier weights in each successive set   (p. 38)
11. The present trend in set training is
    A. to use fewer repetitions in each successive set
    b. to use the same number of repetitions in each successive set

c. to use more repetitions in each successive set   (p. 38)
12. A man who is pressed for time may prefer to use
    a. the multipoundage system   b. a blitz program   C. a split routine (p. 39)
13. Body builders have a tendency to consume a great amount of dietary supplements
    which are high in
    a. carbohydrate   B. protein   c. fat   (p. 7)
14. he condition known as "muscle-bound"
    a. does not exist
    b. is commonly found among weight trainers
    C. is found only among men who train incorrectly   (p. 11)
15. Vigorous exercise
    a. will "sweat out" a cold
    B. does not have any effect on its progress
    c. may make it worse   (p. 11)
16. Circuit training is popular with athletes and the military because
    A. it provides cardiorespiratory stress
    b. it provides muscular stress
    c. it is quick and simple   (p. 36)
17. The rest-pause system
    A. is better for the production of strength than of hypertrophy
    b. is better for the production of hypertrophy than of strength
    c. is equally good for either one   (p. 38)
18. The principle use of a swing bell is
    a. to introduce exercises which cannot be done with a barbell
    b. to introduce exercises which cannot be done with a dumbbell
    C. to introduce variety into the program   (p. 56)
19. The Zinovieff or Oxford technique used in rehabilitation work is simply another
    name for the
    a. light and heavy system   c. multipoundage system
    B. heavy and light system   (p. 34)
20. The "good morning" exercise is a variation of the
    a. the front raise   b. the high pull-up   C. straight-legged dead lift (p. 22)
21. The high pull-up is an excellent exercise for the
    A. trapezius   b. quadriceps   c. spinae erectoris   (p. 15)
22. Many experienced weight lifters consider that the basic exercise for the shoulders is
    a. the curl   C. the press off the back of the neck
    b. the bench press   (p. 24)
23. The forearm supinators and pronators receive excellent exercise from
    a. the flying motion   c. the concentration curl
    B. the Zottman curl   (p. 52)
24. A typical superset combination might consist of
    A. curls and presses   c. squats and dead lifts
    b. supine presses and push-ups   (p. 38)
25. When a hopper is used, the amount of weight that can be employed
    a. is reduced   b. remains the same   C. may be increased   (p. 41)
26. To assist in preventing blacking out
    a. Hyperventilate before a lift
    B. Stay in the squatting position as short a time as possible
    c. Lift the weight slowly and carefully   (p. 29)
27. Anabolic steroids are:
    a. recommended for the use of weight trainers.
    b. are both harmless and widely used.
    C. may have highly undesirable side effects.   (p. 3)
28. Progressive resistance exercise tends
    a. to reduce flexibility   C. to increase flexibility
    b. to have no effect on flexibility   (p. 11)

29. "Overtraining" will
    A. reduce both performance capacity and the ability to resist infections
    b. reduce performance capacity but not the ability to resist infections
    c. reduce the ability to resist infections but not performance capacity   (p. 11)
30. Most of the standardized set of exercises now in general use derive from a book
    written by   (p. 13)
    a. Bob Hoffman   b. Peary Rader   C. Theodor Siebert
31. The exercise program which is based on the theory that muscles should be exercised
    in a large number of different ways is known as
    A. the 1001 exercise system   c. the multipoundage system
    b. the super multiple set system   (p. 30)
32. In order to properly evaluate a program a man should be prepared to stay on it
    a. one month   b. three months   C. six months   (p. 33)
33. Once a certain level of strength is reached, further gains
    a. continue to improve performance   c. hinder performance
    B. do not improve performance   (p. 66)
34. Your girl friend complains of being "flat chested." You should suggest she practice
    A. pull-overs, supine presses, flying motions
    b. half squats, presses, curls
    c. high pull-ups, rowing motion, shoulder shrug   (p. 32)
35. An excellent exercise for the triceps is the   (p. 50)
    a. dumbbell swing   B. Hise deltoid exercise   c. dumbbell high pull-up
36. The present public acceptance of weight training is attributable largely to the
    work of   (p. 1)
    a. Mark H. Berry   B. Thomas L. Delorme   c. David P. Willoughby
37. The practice of weight-training produces
    A. little improvement in cardiorespiratory function
    b. moderate improvement in cardiorespiratory function
    c. great improvement in cardiorespiratory function   (p. 12)
38. The latest exercise system to achieve popularity is the
    a. superset system   C. the spinae erectors and deltoids
    b. multipoundage system   (p. 36)
39. The light and heavy system seem best fitted for the production of
    A. strength   b. hypertrophy   c. definition   (p. 34)
40. The PHA System appears best adapted for the production of
    a. hypertrophy and definition   c. strength and hypertrophy
    B. strength and definition   (p. 38)
41. The primary object of the dumbbell swing is to develop
    a. the biceps and triceps   c. the spinae erectors and deltoids
    b. the trapezius and latissimus dorsi   (p. 49)
42. The average young woman tends to have calves which are too small. To overcome
    this you might prescribe
    a. bent over lateral raises and supine lateral raises
    B. donkey raises and heel raises
    c. front raises and lateral raises   (p. 19-20, 43)
43. The program used by judoka training at the Kodokan stresses use of
    a. barbells   B. dumbbells   c. calisthenics   (p. 72)
44. Most individuals can
    A. press less with dumbbells than with barbells
    b. press the same with dumbbells as with barbells
    c. press more with dumbbells than with barbells   (p. 47)
45. The goal in the blitz system is
    a. to keep the blood in constant circulation
    B. to keep the blood in a limited area
    c. to avoid any influence on the blood

46. A friend asks for an advanced exercise for the triceps. You might suggest
    a. bent arm pull-over   C. French press
    b. high pull-up   (p. 28)
47. The correlation between the girth of the forearm and the strength of the handgrip is
    a. low   B. moderate   c. high   (p. 27)
48. It is generally agreed that the average individual requires each night about
    a. seven hours of sleep   c. nine hours of sleep
    B. eight hours of sleep   (p. 7)
49. According to Higgins, the purpose of weight training for swimmers is to develop
    A. strength   b. bulk   c. definition   (p. 70)
50. Jay Silvester, the best combined shot-put and discus thrower in the world, uses
    A. a light and heavy program   c. a multipoundage program
    b. a heavy and light program   (p. 70)
51. In a normal training routine, the optimal length of rest pauses appears to be about
    a. one minute   b. two minutes   C. three minutes   (p. 6)
52. The front raise with dumbbells is particularly beneficial to the
    A. deltoids   b. triceps   c. biceps   (p. 48)
53. Normally a man should work out
    A. three times a week   c. five times a week
    b. four times a week   (p. 30)
54. However, a man on a split routine might train
    a. four days a week   C. six days a week
    b. five days a week   (p. 39)
55. A man doing a reverse curl should expect to handle about
    a. one third as much as he does in the regular curl
    b. one half as much as he does in the regular curl
    C. two thirds as much as he does in the regular curl   (p. 16)
56. The major portion of the diet should be
    a. protein   B. carbohydrate   c. fat   (p. 7)
57. One of your students desires to exercise his abdominus oblique muscles. You might suggest
    a. the dumbbell swing   C. the side bend
    b. the "good morning" exercise   (p. 51)
58. The training program should provide for
    A. short, frequent rest pauses   c. rest pauses whenever fatigue occurs
    b. long, infrequent rest pauses   (p. 6)
59. In performing dead lifts it is best to
    a. have both hands facing forward
    B. have one hand facing forward and one backward
    c. have both hands facing backward   (p. 21)

TRUE OR FALSE

t F 60. The publishers of magazines on weight training have made substantial contributions to our understanding of the physiology of activity. (p. 29)

t F 61. The AMA Committee on the Medical Aspects of Sports has condemned the half squat as "potentially dangerous to the internal and supporting structures of the knee joint." (p. 19)

T f 62. Technically, no work is accomplished during isometric exercise, even though the exerciser becomes fatigued. (p. 45)

t F 63. John Jesse believes that a training program for weight throwers should concentrate on the development of tremendous overall strength. (p. 70)

T f 64. The AAU disbars any athlete known to have used drugs. (p. 8)

T f 65. In the PHA system, a sequence consists of five or six exercises arranged in such a way that each affects a different part of the body. (p. 36) t F 66. The use of tobacco is extremely deleterious to the development of strength and hypertrophy. (p. 9)

T f 67. Only rarely are body builders outstanding athletes. (p. 62)

t F 68. The athlete may take it as an axiom that "The more strength and hypertrophy the better." (p. 66)

COMPLETION

69. Nutritionists recommend that the daily diet include food from "the basic seven." These are [(1) *milk, cheese, and ice cream;* (2) *meat, fish, poultry, eggs, dried peas, and beans;* (3) *bread, flour, and margarines;* (4) *butter and fortified margarines;* (5) *potatoes and other vegetables and fruits;* (6) *leafy, green and yellow vegetables;* (7) *citrus fruits*]. (p. 7)

70. The international organization governing physique contests is (*Federation International Halterophile et Culturiste*). (p. 64)

71. The results of a program of progressive resistance exercise seems to depend upon the following variables [(1) *stress placed on muscles;* (2) *duration of exercise period;* (3) *frequency of exercise periods*]. (p. 29)

72. The key question in any discussion of the development of muscle is, (*"What can you do with them?"*) (p. 66)

73. One advantage of circuit training is that it may be (*"biased"*) to give specialized work to certain muscle groups. (p. 36)

74. Muscular contraction may be divided into the following types, (*concentric, isometric, lengthening*). (p. 3)

75. The traditional prescription for losing weight is (*low*) resistance and (*high*) repetitions; for gaining weight it is (*high*) resistance and (*low*) repetitions. (p. 9)

76. The disadvantage of going on a strict diet is that one may lose (*muscle tone*) as well as weight. (p. 10)

77. Those who advocate practice of a few heavy exercises for gaining weight emphasize the slogan (*bulk up, train down*). (p. 10)

78. It has been shown that harm may result from massive doses of vitamin (A, D, M). (p. 8)

79. Vitamin supplementation may be required in the case of athletes who (*must make weight*) or who (*train very strenuously*). (p. 8)

80. The bulk craze has caused many body builders to lose sight of the fact that the (*individual measurements must be in proportion*). (p. 59)

81. Use of the straight-arm lateral raise and the straight-arm pull-over is subject to the objection that (*they may cause deltoid strain or overstretch the elbow joint*). (p. 20, 49-50)

82. Few deaths have occurred as a result of weight training. In each case the death was the result of a weight falling on a man during practice of the (*supine press*). (p. 10-11)

83. The reducing diet must contain sufficient (*vitamins and minerals*) but be relatively low in (*calories*). (p. 10)

84. The "overload principle" states that (*strength increases in response to repetitive exercise against progressively increased resistance*). (p. 5)

85. The dangerous point during dead lifting is the period during which the upper body (*is fully flexed*). (p. 21)

86. The basic principle of isokinetic exercise is (*to provide resistance proportional to the input of muscular force and alterations in skeletal levers throughout the range of motion*). (p. 3)

87. The general rule for breathing during weight training is to (*inhale*) while contracting the muscles and (*exhale*) while relaxing them. (p. 29)

88. Some of the older weight trainers are prejudiced against the use of dumbbells on the grounds (*that they make a man "stiff"*). (p. 47)

89. The purpose of the "cheat" in a cheating exercise is to (*get the weight past the "sticking point"*). (p. 35)

90. Men who find it difficult to gain must show the following qualities if they are to achieve success: (*open-mindedness, a readiness to experiment, and willingness to stick with a schedule long enough to determine its potential*). (p. 33)

91. All advanced training methods depend upon the following principle (*increasing the amount of stress placed upon the body within the given training period*). (p. 33)

92. The basic principle in the heavy and light system is (*to keep working the muscles against near maximal resistance*). (p. 34)

93. Some instructors contend that the position assumed in the bent over rowing motion should be avoided because (*the long lever and the weight of the upper body and resistance place a great strain on the lower back*). (p. 25)

94. In practicing the Zottman curl, the amount of weight that can be handled will be controlled by (*the strength that can be exerted in the reverse curl*). (p. 52)

95. Too much protein in the diet may leave an (*acid residue*) which throws an extra load on (*the kidneys*). (p. 8)

96. The rowing motion to the waist appears to have more effect on the (*latissimus dorsi*) muscle than does the rowing motion to the chest. (p. 25)

97. In performing POBNs it is essential that the weight not be allowed to (*drop on the vertebrae of the neck*). (p. 24)

98. It has been said that "More people believe more bunk about (*food and nutrition*) than any other single topic in the health field." (p. 7)

99. If a muscle is worked regularly the following changes will occur: (*a permanent increase in the number of capillaries; the ability of the muscle to assimilate nutritive materials will improve; the size and functional power of the cells will improve*). (p. 45)

100. In routine dumbbell training, most trainers seem to prefer (*alternate*) exercises. (p. 47)

Name Index

Subject Index